The Hope in Our Scars is at c  ;ing. Aimee Byrd pulls no punche 'the church, both corporately and ‚ has wounded and marred the very people it should nurture, leaving them scarred. And yet in the midst of that searing honesty, there is radiant hope, for she always sees the church, and ourselves within it, as also and always the beloved bride of Christ, who has forever wedded his story to ours, and by whose wounds our wounds are healed. In an age when so many are turning away disillusioned or deconstructing their faith, *The Hope in Our Scars* offers a recovery of vision and confidence; a call to tell and retell our own stories as honestly as possible and so renew our intimacy with Christ and one another.

—**MALCOLM GUITE,** poet, priest, life fellow
of Girton College Cambridge

This is a book for the bruised ones, for the smoldering wicks, for the disillusioned. With clarity and grace, Aimee Byrd shows that there can be beauty even in the midst of brokenness and that the true church of Christ is a place of healing, restoration, and hope. A beautiful testimony of compassion and resilience.

—**KRISTIN KOBES DU MEZ,** *New York Times*
bestselling author of *Jesus and John Wayne*

Aimee's newest book strains toward hope and beauty even as she honestly acknowledges the pain and perils of navigating today's fraught ecclesial landscape. Once again, she offers compelling new thoughts, but it's her vulnerability that draws me in and inspires me to keep my heart open and hopeful, not least because of the one whose scars paved the resurrection path.

—**CHUCK DEGROAT,** author of *When Narcissism
Comes to Church* and professor of pastoral care
and executive director of the Clinical Counseling
Program at Western Theological Seminary

What a gift this book is! The beauty of Aimee's faith shines through the ugliness of her story—reminding us why the church is still worth fighting for and giving us the wisdom we need to keep fighting for it. You will want this book for your friends, family, and church. But most of all, you will want it for yourself.

—**BETH ALLISON BARR,** James Vardaman
Professor of History at Baylor University

Aimee Byrd is an epic storyteller, and she tell us a story, her story, many people's story. It's a story of affliction, disappointment, despair, and shame—and how to grow closer to God out of it. Aimee testifies to how God is faithful even when the people who claim to speak for God are evidently not. Replete with scriptural reflections and her own personal experiences, Aimee shows readers that our spiritual and emotional scars are painful memories etched into our skin, but those scars can also be signs of healing and getting stronger.

—**MICHAEL F. BIRD,** deputy principal at
Ridley College, Melbourne, Australia

Giving voice to the questions many hurting people are asking, Byrd ultimately directs our eyes to the answer, the one to whom the church belongs, Christ himself. As she discloses her own story of God's pursuit even in the midst of deep pain, she also invites readers to name their own story so that they can begin to see how it is already being caught up into God's grand and good narrative. With the Song of Songs as her primary muse, she dialogues with Scripture and a diverse range of scholars to offer practical advice and, most importantly, hope for the possibility of restoration.

—**AMY PEELER,** professor of New Testament,
Wheaton College, priest, and author of
Women and the Gender of God

THE HOPE IN OUR SCARS

THE HOPE IN OUR SCARS

FINDING THE BRIDE OF CHRIST IN
THE UNDERGROUND OF DISILLUSIONMENT

AIMEE BYRD

ZONDERVAN
REFLECTIVE

ZONDERVAN REFLECTIVE

The Hope in Our Scars
Copyright © 2024 by Aimee Byrd

Published in Grand Rapids, Michigan, by Zondervan. Zondervan is a registered trademark of The Zondervan Corporation, L.L.C., a wholly owned subsidiary of HarperCollins Christian Publishing, Inc.

Requests for information should be addressed to customercare@harpercollins.com.

Zondervan titles may be purchased in bulk for educational, business, fundraising, or sales promotional use. For information, please email SpecialMarkets@Zondervan.com.

ISBN 978-0-310-15716-8 (audio)

Library of Congress Cataloging-in-Publication Data

Names: Byrd, Aimee, 1975- author.
Title: The hope in our scars : finding the bride of Christ in the underground of disillusionment / Aimee Byrd.
Description: Grand Rapids, Michigan : Zondervan, 2024.
Identifiers: LCCN 2023040948 | ISBN 9780310157144 (paperback) | ISBN 9780310157151 (ebook)
Subjects: LCSH: Shame--Religious aspects--Christianity. | Hope--Religious aspects --Christianity. | Disillusion (Philosophy) | BISAC: RELIGION / Christian Ministry / Discipleship | RELIGION / Christian Living / Spiritual Growth
Classification: LCC BT714 .B97 2024 | DDC 234/.25--dc23/eng/20240124
LC record available at https://lccn.loc.gov/2023040948

Published in association with Don Gates of the literary agency The Gates Group, www.the -gates-group.com.

Cover design: Thinkpen Design
Interior design: Kait Lamphere

Printed in the United States of America
24 25 26 27 28 LBC 5 4 3 2 1

To my three Byrdies as you are flying out of the nest:
Solanna, Zaidee, and Haydn

* * *

You've already endured scars. I pray that this book—and
more so, your dad and I—will help you see what's real.
May your scars bear hope for the powerful testimony
that they tell—the beauty in the mending of Christ filling
us with his own body broken and given for us.

CONTENTS

INTRO

BEAUTY RISES

Every person comes to church with a story. And expectations. When things go well, our stories are drawn out of us and given new light in the reality and beauty of the gospel, and our expectations for church life are transformed beyond what we could have even known to ask for. We find that we are part of a much bigger, overarching story that has us on a dynamic trajectory together. The story is that God is preparing our souls for love. He is inviting us to share in the Father's great love for the Son by the Spirit.

As our personal stories unfold and weave with the stories of our brothers and sisters in the faith under this metanarrative, we hold them together as a testimony to where we've come from, what we've been through, and the beauty Christ is inviting us into together through them. In this, we find freedom in belonging to Christ. Freedom to be known, to love, to give, and to sacrifice for one another on our way. Freedom to promote one another's holiness and goodness. Freedom to share our struggles and pain. Freedom to confess our sin.

And freedom to seek beauty together, which helps us to see clearly and reminds us of our trajectory—communion with the triune God and one another.

But it doesn't happen that way for many of us. It didn't for me.

It used to feel virtuous to say that I went to church. Now when I say it to my unbelieving friends and acquaintances, there's a bit of embarrassment behind it. I feel the need to add, "Really though, I'm not one of those angry people you see on the internet or rushing the Capitol building." And then I pray to God that I'm telling the truth (about the angry part). The truth is, some things happening in the church should provoke our anger. And the truth is, I have been fighting to love Christ's church. I thought I found genuine belonging for a good while. But I was left disillusioned as I attempted to understand the spiritual abuse I was experiencing. It is both curious and tragic that the abuse arose when I tried to make sense of discipleship as a woman in the church.

Many of you are like me. Maybe spiritual abuse didn't lead to your disillusionment with the church. But a lot of us are trying to make sense of discipleship and spiritual formation. What does it look like? Where does it happen? How is it significant? Where do I fit in? There is a lot we need to sort out. Our own expectations going in are often part of the problem. And it's all too easy to lose sight of Christ.

The church has always prided herself on missions—sending people out to share the good news and bringing new Christians into the community of faith. But what if "the church" is the mission field? The church is struggling with a major PR problem.* She has lost her respect and significance in the world and in local communities. She's racked with scandals of fraud, abuse, and cover-up. She's mocked on television. She looks like a complete bigot to outsiders. We continue to see racism, misogyny, and other stories of marginalization and hate *in the church.* Our youth are aging out and saying, "No thanks."† There is a whole movement of previously committed Christians who are deconstructing their faith. And then there is a rising class of people known as the "nones" who aren't committed to any faith affiliation at all.‡ With scandal, cover-up, and hatred as our witness, can we blame them?

Inside our church doors, hurting people are struggling to see Christ in their lives. Instead of giving the world a beautiful picture of Christ's bride and a glimpse of his love for us, many see disillusionment, despair, and abuse. Look at our scars. Look at the scars on the church. How did we get here? Church isn't what many of us thought it would be. We can't seem to live in the real world that we sing about on Sunday mornings. It seems so disconnected.

If Christianity has all the answers, why is there so much ugliness in the church? Having gone through my own

---

* See Aaron Earls, "Pastors and Churches Face Historic Lack of Trust," Lifeway Research, Insights Faith and Culture (website), July 12, 2022, https://research.lifeway.com/2022/07/12/pastors-and-churches-face-historic-lack-of-trust/?carid=0a284027–3d05–4aa6–9bd9-c0d1b6d1e2e5&profile=lifewayresearch&network=twitter.

† See Aaron Earls, "Most Teenagers Drop Out of Church When They Become Young Adults," Lifeway Research, Culture (website), January 15, 2019, https://research.lifeway.com/2019/01/15/most-teenagers-drop-out-of-church-as-young-adults/.

‡ See Gregory A. Smith, "About Three-in-Ten U.S. Adults Are Now Religiously Unaffiliated," Pew Research Center, Dec. 14, 2021, https://www.pewresearch.org/religion/2021/12/14/about-three-in-ten-u-s-adults-are-now-religiously-unaffiliated/.

disillusionment, I wrote this book as a plea to look at what's real. I'm fighting to love Christ's church because she is *Christ's* church. The apostle John teaches us that discipleship may not look the way we think. What are our expectations as we come to church? Why does Christ call us together to worship him this way, and what is he doing in the process? Furthermore, why can't we seem to get this right? Scripture testifies that the church was already having problems in its infancy. The letters to the seven churches in Revelation are sobering to say the least. But as John begins revealing his vision, the way he describes himself teaches us a lot about discipleship in the church:

> I, John, your brother and partner in the affliction, kingdom, and endurance that are in Jesus, was on the island called Patmos because of the word of God and the testimony of Jesus. (Rev. 1:9)

When I came across this verse for the I-don't-know-how-manyeth time in my life, I finally paused. Look at that. Look at what John calls himself as a fellow disciple. He is a brother and a partner. That is what we are *for* each other: siblings and allies. And look at the context. Maybe this whole thing we call church life is not what we thought going in. We are siblings and partners in affliction, kingdom, and endurance that are in Jesus. That framework can help us with our struggles in the church today. Here is our expectation. And here is our hope.

Why is affliction part of discipleship? What if God is using our disillusionment as a tool to direct us to him? What if he wants to give his bride the beautiful, good, and true?

John shows us where we are headed, what the endgame is: participation in the covenantal, spousal union with Christ. We practice this together now as the church as our souls are in training for the love that is waiting for us.

The triune God is inviting us into the incomprehensible beauty of his church. *The Hope in Our Scars* will direct us to see Christ among the chaos. Our imaginations will open as his Spirit shows us through his Word, and through our own adversities, that things are not as they seem. Is this not what Revelation, as well as the whole of Scripture, teaches us? We are living as the wilderness bride between this age and the age to come. Like the Israelites journeying to the land of Canaan that the Lord promised to give them, we too are on our way out of the wilderness. But we are headed to something even more unfathomable than the land flowing with milk and honey that the Israelite spies observed. We are on our way to the heavenizing of earth, the union of heaven and earth. At times, we can't see it. We have our eyes set on obstacles that seem like giants. Often, they are within the church—and its leadership.

Like the woman in the Song of Songs (Song 3:6; 8:5) and the woman in Revelation (Rev. 12:6), we are the wilderness bride, looking forward to our consummation with the Lord when we will be the bride assembled and ruling with him on this new heavens and earth, the mountain of the Lord. Our golden age is not here and now. God is conditioning us. It is breaking in. As his wilderness bride, we are partners in affliction, kingdom, and endurance as our caring God is preparing our souls for love.

Because beauty rises. What is true of the incarnate Christ

is true of his people. As a church, we are a manifestation of Christ's bride to a groomless world—to those who do not know the spousal love of Christ. Some of us need to be reminded of this. And some will be hearing it for the first time. This vision of what is real and the invitation into it is a call to receive and reciprocate God's self-gift of unitive love. It summons us to life together. It stirs our affections, ignites our imaginations, and directs our desires. As we covenantally participate in this summons together, our churches' witness proclaims a belonging that supersedes all earthly shadows.

Whether you are in the mission field of the church, wounded, disillusioned, questioning, deconstructing, or just trying to figure out what faith and church is all about, I want to show you something beautiful and enduring. This book is an invitation to what's real. So we need to look at our scars and the testimony they bear. We will face affliction, imagine God's kingdom, and talk about how we endure together to behold what is coming for us. It's a book about Christ and his love, Christ and his bride. And it's a book about stories—our stories and how they all come together.

PART 1

PARTNERS IN AFFLICTION

DISILLUSIONED DISCIPLES

Part of being a successful, launching adult meant being in a family that belongs to a church. That is how I always envisioned it. That's what I was going to do.

My parents lost their way, somehow, and it imploded during my high school years. We weren't connected to the families and leaders inside our church and it was palpable—the sense of belonging but not belonging. Worshipers at a distance. My parents divorced when I was sixteen. How could this happen to a family of faith who was part of a church? Where was the fruit of worshiping together with all these believers? Was there ever any substance to it?

We disintegrated as a family. And from the church.

I took this as my invitation not to be the picture-perfect Christian teen and left that all behind for a while.

The Christian morals used to raise me seemed to all go out the window when my parents split. We were broken. It didn't pan out. No one in the church was there for us when our lives were falling apart. No one reached out. We faded. It was convenient, then, to use that pain and brokenness to my advantage as a teenager. You know, live it up a little before becoming more serious about that whole Christianity thing.

I was going to get serious about it, down the road and all. In my mind, I still loved Jesus and would come back to him when it was important. But he came for me.

This book unfolded as I tried to learn about discipleship in adulthood. In other words, if we are to take this being a Christian thing seriously in adult life, what does that look like? If Christianity is true, what can we hold fast to when we don't want to act like it? And how do we grow into maturity? I became an author accidentally while trying to figure all this out, writing books I couldn't find in my own search for meaning as a disciple. I wrote from a place of loneliness as a thinking young woman in the church, trying to find a space and communicate. Each book was another step in trying to make sense of what I was seeing and experiencing, while asking the theological questions behind it. Ultimately, Christian discipleship is a search for beauty, significance, and where our true longings are met.

I thought I was entitled to press pause on this search during the last half of my teenage years. In reality, I was only looking in the wrong places. But while I was marginalizing God, God came for me.

LIVING ON A PRAYER

Deep down, I knew that I belonged to Christ. This knowledge was a comfort and, sadly, something to take advantage of, as my theology allowed me to. I "prayed the prayer" at eight years old. You know the one, the one that asks Jesus into your heart and means you've locked him in with a free, nonrefundable ticket to heaven. "Once saved, always saved" was the slogan. I thought it was a memory verse from the Bible somewhere. But it was more than that for me. I can't remember a time when I didn't love Jesus. My parents instilled it in me—Jesus's love for me, for us. I treasured that. Wondered in it. So at eight years old, when my Vacation Bible School teacher told me I wasn't "saved" without praying the prayer, it processed as a little disturbing that nothing before that day in my relationship with God seemed to count before locking it in with the right words. Didn't he hear all those prayers for the first eight years? Phew, praise God for VBS and the woman with the blue eyeshadow and curiously painted on eyebrows to show me the right way! It didn't feel any different though. I mean, I was still judging this woman's cosmetic choices. Good thing I prayed the prayer.

I had my ticket to heaven, and we seemed to have the perfect family until it all unraveled. People looked up to us. We enjoyed one another, did fun and creative things together, took vacations, showed affection, had friends, and went to church. Our yard was the neighborhood hangout. Dad often organized obstacle courses and timed us as we ran through. Mom taught aerobics to the neighborhood housewives. My parents instilled Christian morals in us and, more importantly, a habit of prayer. They showed us love.

Children don't realize all that their parents take with them into marriage. I assumed mine had all their crap together. But they were married so young, at a mere nineteen and seventeen years old, with me in utero. They each had their own unpacked trauma. Looking back, it makes more sense why they were wary about getting too involved in church. But that's their story to tell. As much as I was into loving Jesus, their divorce and subsequent break from church* began to reveal something off in my own heart. I took that ticket to heaven and put it in my pocket for a while. Checking all the boxes didn't seem to be working for us, so why not rebel a little bit? Isn't that the expectation for a teenage child of divorce?

A family like ours didn't belong in church. And I didn't know what it meant to belong to my family anymore either. As the world of driving opened, my car also became a symbol of my transience, functioning as a closet for schlepping between houses. Teenagers are looking for belonging, divorced parents or not. We all seem to think we are the only ones scrambling to find it. I sought it in popularity and teenage affection. As Tom Petty put it, I loved Jesus and my boyfriend too.†

At the beginning of my junior year of college, God got my attention again. Now, don't think that I completely forgot him. College-party Aimee was still praying, reading the Bible now and then, and considering herself a Christian. Some of my values were changing though, even as I knew how to speak

---

* This is not the case now. God is continuing to work in all of our lives.
† I'm mixing the lyrics a bit here.

the language and identify as "saved." So when greeted by a Campus Crusade for Christ* member sitting dutifully at her display table in front of the dining hall, asking the notorious, "How do you know if you will go to heaven when you die?" I knew the answer. The formula. As a matter of fact, I was counting on it. Holding it in my pocket to cash in later.

Not much later, you see. As I said, I had every intention to return to church as a responsible adult. But college wasn't for responsible adults! I was having fun, experimenting with alternate realities. Not one to put stock in charismatic experiences, I'm a bit uncomfortable sharing how God got ahold of me. I was out partying with my friends. He was supposed to stay in my pocket. It wasn't a voice from heaven. It wasn't a vision in a dream. But it had to be the Holy Spirit because it was a conviction and mindfulness about the person I was becoming and the life I was living juxtaposed to my confession as a Christian. Don't get me wrong, I had standards that set me apart from others. I wasn't like *them*. All of a sudden, the hypocrisy and foolishness was clear. My affections did a U-turn. Suddenly, God became urgent. And it became clearer that living my life for him instead of for myself required more learning about who he was than a handful of catch phrases and a ticket in my pocket. There had to be more to hold fast to than a prayer I said when I was eight. I needed to learn more about his character, his essence even. I wanted to *know* him.

So I went to church. A Southern Baptist one, since it was familiar and comfortable.

Not the bad kind of Baptists that my mom escaped at

---

* Their name has now changed to Cru. Much edgier.

seventeen, mind you—the fundamentalists who said she couldn't wear jeans, play cards, or listen to secular music. I went to the more reasonable ones who recognized legalism and also wanted to be good people. This denominational affiliation brought not only belonging but safety. This is how I saw it.*

You would think that a nineteen-year-old university student taking initiative to go to church all alone in her college town would catch the attention of its members. Those were my expectations: not to be singled out and celebrated immediately for being there, but for some of the mature Christians to take notice that a young woman was seeking Christian community—from a church, not merely among her peers in a campus parachurch organization—and maybe invite me to lunch, to a study group, or whatever adulting Christians do. Show me the ropes. Teach me thy ways. Instead, in introducing myself to one of the greeters at the door, ready to do this whole living the Christian life thing now, she reciprocated with a smile, an "Isn't that nice?" and a jar of jelly. That whole season of going to church was quite lonely. I turned to the local Christian bookstore, the Gospel Shoppe, for my education.

This was my second disillusionment with a church. At the time, I didn't realize these were wounds on my soul that targeted my value and that of Christ's body. But I had a new resolve this time, a commitment to know God better. Love was beckoning me.

---

* I know this is dripping with irony. While writing this, the Department of Justice has begun an investigation into the Southern Baptist Convention. This transpired shortly after a third-party group, Guidepost Solutions, released a report revealing how high-ranking SBC officials horrifically handled reports of sexual abuse cases from 2000 to 2020. It shows a pattern of intimidation, silencing, and neglecting victims and those who advocated for them.

WHAT'S YOUR STORY?

What do we do when church isn't what we thought it was? Many find that instead of the church helping us to make sense of the world, we can't make sense of the church. Some never find a sense of belonging. It's just a place, as theologian Mike Bird calls it, where we go to listen to a concert and a TED talk.[1] Some who want to go deeper in the church's community life can't seem to penetrate the inner circles. Many are burned out from serving in programs that are supposed to make church relevant while never being ministered to. The growing number who do come with vexing questions are treated as "repugnant cultural others."[2] We see that the church is often associated with political parties over people. American evangelicalism, in particular, has strong alliances with white Christian nationalism, patriarchy, racism, and abuse cover-up.[3] What is happening? All this makes people wonder: Is God who we thought he was? Where do we belong? What do we believe?

The Holy Spirit grabbed my affections on that random evening while I was partying with friends. And I was just naive enough to think that the next and final step was to get my theology right (not that I was sophisticated enough to use the word *theology*)—to know God truly in order to worship him well, and, you know, turn out good. Find a good man. Be a good wife. Raise my kids right. Not screw things up. Thinking that church would be a community that would help me and my future family make sense of the world, I looked to the church for answers to the big questions and to help me learn what questions to ask. After stumbling through this search for what

I thought church ought to be, I find myself suffering from disillusionment alongside many others in the church who have
high hopes. What do we do with these wounds? Can we look at
them together and talk about them? I'll share more of my story
as we go, but hopefully mine has ignited questions about your
own relationship with Christ and his church. What brought
you in? What kept you in? Is church what you thought it was?
Where are your affections, and what do you truly know about
God? Where are you headed, and who do you want to be with?

I used to think it was too self-absorbed to tell my story. Part
of that thinking was the culture of the Presbyterian church
tradition I have spent the last seventeen years in. Wanting to
put the proper focus on God, I devalued the testimonies of how
God works in people's actual lives. I didn't want to become one
of those who are "psychologizing the faith," "turning inward,"
or "man-centered." That meant not acknowledging that God
created us with a psyche. Yet he summons us holistically. Our
stories matter to God. He's made us storied people. Our storied selves come together on Sundays, and we are recalibrated
through the simple elements of worship—the call to worship,
confession of sin, absolution, singing, praying, preached word,
baptism, Lord's Supper, and benediction—as we find our place
in the reality of God's great story, which reminds us of our
true belonging, significance, and value. God isn't only after
our brains. He's beckoning all our senses as embodied people,
igniting our imaginations and sense of wonder, connecting our
confession of who he is with the cloud of witnesses that have
gone before us, and teaching us about his gift of true freedom
in belonging.

Sharing our stories is part of this process. It does something incredible. It's generative. Through our stories, we come to know not only one another but also ourselves—and even God. When we share our stories, we are sharing our very selves with one another. And when we can do that with trusted people, things come out of us that we didn't realize we'd been holding in. We need partners in affliction, people who will bear witness to where we are and what we've experienced and still stay in the room with us. We also need to hear others speak into our version of events, as we've been silently self-narrating. We can't see our own selves and stories alone—we weren't meant to.[4]

As confidants actively listen to our stories, they make connections with their own stories. They too are encouraged to share. We help one another name our experiences, process them, celebrate and lament in them, see Christ at work through them, remind us of our trajectory, and encourage one another with the tools we need to endure. We help one another draw out our deepest wants and recognize how Christ is both the end and the implanter of our inmost desires. As philosopher D. C. Schindler explains, building from Soren Kierkegaard, "Love *presupposes* precisely what it gives."[5] "To exist, as creatures, is therefore to rise up, so to speak, to meet this love."[6] We rise together and "go with" one another even in our absence, as we walk in the unitive love that we indwell.

What is your story? We will continue to revisit this question because we all have more to draw out than we recognize. Sharing our story is a vulnerable and brave act. We work hard to cover up our wounds and move on, not realizing the impact they make in our relationships and in our own bodies. Facing them and sharing them is an act of hope because we see that things are not the way they are supposed to be. Hope—real hope, which isn't caught up in sentimentality or wishful thinking—reveals unmet longings. Many do not hope because, as therapist Adam Young put it, "hope is agonizing."[7] We see and suffer this gap between the expectation of how things will be and where we find ourselves now. But if we spend time facing our wounds, doing the brave work of inviting others to see them with the intimacy that brings, and joining together with God in their healing, the testimonies of our scars will reveal the substance of our faith.

The overarching story is unfolding. It isn't only two-thousand-year-old good news. Resurrections are happening all around us every day. Out of our own stories and the questions we wrestled with through disillusionment, we discover that God is more than we thought he was. He wants us to ask questions and tell our stories so that we can see how intimately present he is. He uses our disillusionment to show himself to us. By an act of grace, he reveals the counterfeit belonging we were searching for satisfaction in. Christ is better than what we think success is. Christ is better than what we think freedom is. Christ is better than any acceptance or influence we think we have. He is better than the security we hold in checking the boxes. He is better than our image of the perfect Christian. By turning to him while facing disillusionment, we learn of matters that transcend our sanitized ideals. Beauty, goodness, and truth cannot be reduced to our versions of them. Much to our bewilderment, rather than uploading all the information we need to know to be good Christians into our minds, he invites us behind the curtain into the holy of holies. In telling our stories, we learn that our disillusionment isn't only with the church; it is with ourselves and what we thought Christ was doing with us in the first place.

WHERE ELSE DO WE GO?

There were disillusioned disciples in the Bible as well. They found that the One in whom they were putting their hope said some pretty weird things. He wasn't what they expected. Things got awkward when everyone in the synagogue, who were hanging on his every word, heard Jesus give a message about his body that sounded an awful lot like cannibalism (John 6:53–58). How were they to understand this? Why wasn't Jesus explaining the spiritual meaning to them? Many of his own disciples began murmuring, "This teaching is hard. Who can accept it?" (v. 60). Instead of making it easier, Jesus then tells them, "This is why I told you that no one can come to me unless it is granted to him by the Father" (v. 65). *Wait*—that's his explanation after saying that we do not have life in ourselves if we do not eat his flesh and drink his blood? After saying he was the actual manna that comes down from heaven? *What?* Who can understand this? Who can accept it? How are we to evangelize with this? How does it actually help us? Is Jesus really the Messiah, or is he some crazy person claiming to be God? And we are to feed on his flesh? Who are we following here? This isn't what I signed up for!

Many of his disciples couldn't accept it and "turned back and no longer accompanied him" (v. 66). We can only imagine the disillusionment the twelve who remained were facing.

"So Jesus said to the Twelve, 'You don't want to go away too, do you?' Simon Peter answered, 'Lord, to whom will we go? You have the words of eternal life. We have come to believe and know that you are the Holy One of God'" (vv. 67–69). Is God who we thought he was? No, he is far greater and far more incomprehensible. Like the disciples who answered him, we still have a lot of questions. Can we get the answers from somewhere else? Better people, maybe? Better leaders? To whom will we go?

Plenty of churches do not deserve that name. As these twelve disciples are representative roots of the churches that will be planted, the next thing Jesus says alludes to this: "'Didn't I choose you, the Twelve? Yet one of you is a devil'" (v. 70). Okay, Jesus, you keep compounding our confusion and disillusionment by adding more hard things to accept! Why don't you expose him now and take him out of the inner circle? Why allow a devil as one of the Twelve? Why did you choose him, and what does that even mean now in this context?

These are hard things.

Who can know the mind of God? Even from our present perspective on this side of the resurrection, having knowledge of his crucifixion, the institution of the Eucharist, and our need for union with Christ so that we are called the body of Christ, we continue to have much to learn from the mysteries impregnated in Christ's words in the synagogue. Obviously, Jesus is not teaching cannibalism. But he is teaching something terrifyingly unimaginable. It is terrifying in the true sense of the word—terrible enough to cause us "to shake."[8] Our need for him is this great, this dire, this close. We don't just need his teaching or his friendship, but his very flesh and blood. What he offers is unimaginable to our limited understanding—all of him! He doesn't only have the words of eternal life; he is the *person* of eternal life.

He is the God who doesn't just tell us where to go or whom to follow. He *is* where to go. He is reality. He is the beginning and the end. *To whom will we go?* But in going, we will encounter devils. We are not even to have our eyes on the Twelve. We look to them only as they point to him. Jesus doesn't try to turn their disillusionment into perfect understanding. No, they are to take in the hard things because they will face hard things. And they aren't ready to learn it all yet. Accepting the ambiguity in the hard things is part of preparing their souls for love. There will be affliction. Our hope bears scars. And his disciples are to remain in him through it as they seek true food and true drink. There is a resurrection coming (v. 54–57). Beauty rises.

LEARNING TOGETHER

If we are going to talk about disillusioned disciples, what is a disciple to begin with? It's a notably Christian word. But it wasn't always associated with Christianity. We learn in Acts, "The disciples were first called Christians at Antioch" (Acts 11:26). The Jewish rabbinic tradition was passed down through discipleship. Jewish disciples chose a prominent rabbi to study under. Their instruction included a lot of instructional teaching, but more than that too. Choosing represented a big commitment in rabbinic culture in which the disciple would continuously accompany the rabbi, observing everything about him with the aim of becoming a teacher of their own disciples. Theologian Hans Kvalbein elaborates, "The highest hope of a student in a rabbinic 'school' was to become a rabbi like his own teacher. The rabbis tried to educate disciples that in their turn might become rabbis and pass the traditions on to new disciples who could become teachers for still a new generation."[9]

Disciples are learners who become teachers. The writer of Hebrews works from this understanding when he says things such as, "Although by this time you ought to be teachers, you need someone to teach you the basic principles of God's revelation again. You need milk, not solid food" (Heb. 5:12). The disciples in John 6 who walked away from Jesus when they saw that his teaching was hard chose to no longer commit to discipleship under him. It may appear, then, that the Twelve chose Jesus. Good on them. But Jesus adds another teaching that is hard to understand. He reminds them that unlike the Jewish rabbinic tradition, they didn't choose him to study under. He chose them! Although they have the agency to reject him, he is the one who calls his disciples. We hear this again in John 15:16, "You did not choose me, but I chose you. I appointed you to go and produce fruit and that your fruit should remain, so that whatever you ask the Father in my name, he will give you." The one doing the choosing is different than typical discipleship in the rabbinic tradition. And what an amazing promise is attached to it—enduring fruit and access to the Father through him! Discipleship isn't merely about studying under a teacher or becoming a teacher. Christian discipleship is *with*ness. And it's transformative.

Another difference is that in Christian discipleship we are all disciples of the same person. As Jesus said, "But you are not to be called 'Rabbi,' because you have one Teacher, and you are all brothers and sisters" (Matt. 23:8). We are all disciples of Christ. In fellowship, we join him in making more disciples of Christ. He commissioned his disciples:

> Jesus came near and said to them, "All authority has been given to me in heaven and on earth. Go, therefore, and make disciples of all nations, baptizing them in the name of the Father and of the Son and of the Holy Spirit, teaching them to observe everything I have commanded you. And remember, I am with you always, to the end of the age." (Matt. 28:18–20)

They are sent out to the whole world to invite disciples into Christ's kingdom through baptism and his teaching. "All nations are invited to this new fellowship. And therefore all disciples are called to this mission."[10]

FOXES IN THE VINEYARD

John identifies himself in Revelation in the way Jesus taught his disciples. He isn't above his readers. He is their partner and brother. Christian disciples are learners who become teachers *to* and *with* one another, not *over* others. And we are siblings and partners in affliction, kingdom, and endurance in Jesus. That first one—affliction—is a doozy.

In his Great Commission, Jesus promises and comforts his disciples that he is with them always. This picture of discipleship is exciting. We wouldn't expect conflict and agony, then, in the church. Even as we are proclaiming and joining the kingdom of God, and even as Christ is with us through his Spirit, we suffer. We suffer in the same ways unbelievers do: our bodies are breaking down unto death, our hearts get broken, we are insecure, anxious, and we go through tribulations. Christians suffer affliction of all kinds. In a sense, Jesus tells us to expect to suffer more than unbelievers. He says, "Calculate the cost" (Luke 14:28). He suffered affliction. As we become more experienced with affliction, we learn something that you can't teach in the classroom about the spousal love of God. I know that sounds strange but stay with me.

I shared the beginnings of my story of church disillusionment, but it gets worse. As my writing gained readership and presented opportunities to speak, some people were not happy with my message of investing in women and encouraging their agency as disciples. Church officers in my former denomination, among others, continuously harassed and targeted me with reviling behavior, plotting schemes to spread the message that I am dangerous to the church. Dangerous. To the church. We are now escalating further on the scale of church harm and spiritual abuse. For this section, I want to focus on sharing about the effects of this harm as it reveals disillusionment not only for the one being wounded, as we expect. The harm also reveals disillusionment in the ones we go to for help—the leaders who are supposed to direct us to Christ's love and care. And it reveals something is very off in the heart of the church.

It's understood that there are jerks on the internet and

even in the church. We can't whack all the moles. But the qualifications for church office exist for a good reason. I sought help in my church and denomination regarding these church officers. But one has to wonder why the responsibility is left in the hands of the wounded. These leaders' abuse was ongoing, public behavior. During a two-year process within the denomination, I often faced disillusionment as my personhood and dignity were reduced, the basics of care were lacking, abusive leaders had little to no accountability, troubling theology about men and women was exposed and multiplying, and all the while the victims continued to pick up the tab. The formal process to confront abuse left me unable to tell my own story. Before going through this spiritual abuse, I didn't understand trauma. It's an extreme betrayal and violation of trust when the shepherds accountable before God to love and care for the sheep leave you exposed to abuse and then use the process of church order to keep you under it. It makes you wonder what these "men of God" really believe. About love. About power. About community and belonging.

I couldn't understand why the experience was so incredibly painful. I thought myself tougher than that. Logically, I knew it was wrong. I'm a fighter and a truth seeker. Why was I so weak? Why couldn't I get over it? Why was it affecting me physiologically? My body was weary, anxious, sick, depressed. I couldn't sleep, couldn't read. My brain was foggy. I could barely pay attention to what my own kids were saying to me. The ordeal consumed me. And each time I endured another step of the process, the waves of trauma came crashing back.[11]

So I know something about disillusionment in the church. I know how scary it can be to take yourself to a church after these experiences. There's a lot of loss—in relationships, trust, what we thought we knew about church, and even hope. But those who are wounded by the church must face their disillusionment. Too often those in leadership, as well as all those comfortably unaffected in the pews, don't face their own disillusionment with what the church is called to, especially when this disillusionment is juxtaposed to the belief systems and power systems they are operating under.

Several things are helping me get through it, even as I am still processing it all, working to heal, and fighting to love Christ's church. One that I am going to introduce to you now is seeing and entering into that love through reading the Song of Songs. I believe that what the whole church needs in this time of disillusionment is to learn how to read the Song together. The early church fathers referred to the Song of Songs as the "holy of holies of Scripture."[12] If you want to have the most intimate encounter with Christ in his Word, go to the Song. In it, we have a dynamic picture of Christ and his bride, the church. From the Song's conception until the twentieth century, the church read it as an allegory of Christ's love for the church as well as for the soul of every believer. And it has ministered to me to be able to go there, where I can see Christ's words to me and am given words and agency to speak to him. Through the Song I really began to understand the absolute wonder of the hope in our scars, to see how beauty rises. In it we see the whole overarching story of Christ's love for his people—this is what it is all about. In a sense, all of Scripture is sung in the Song. It's the Bible in concentrate. It's the overarching story. As we see its lyrics echoed throughout Scripture, the texts activate one another, enhancing (not changing!) the meaning. I want to show you a little exercise in this as it relates to affliction.

Immediately following a section in the Song where the man is beckoning the lovesick woman's voice, wanting to see her face, with what can be read as a gospel/springtime/ wedding invitation,[13] the woman gives a curious response.

Catch the foxes for us—
the little foxes that ruin the vineyards—
for our vineyards are in bloom. (Song 2:15)

I know, I know, the language of the Song can sound a bit weird and out of place. I've come to love that about it. Here, we experience the tension between the "already" of this true invitation with the Bridegroom breaking in and the "not-yet" of our consummation. The woman teaches us that reality is complex. Think of what a gift this is: here we are in the holy of holies of Scripture, where we can experience the presence of Christ with us in the most intimate place in his Word. Here we are getting behind the veil, our senses aroused to his love with a taste of what is to come. He invites her to "come," describing spring in bloom as their love is in bloom. And yet it's all empty sentimental platitudes if we let ourselves pervert it into mere fantasy.

It's real.

And so is the fact that our preparation to get there can be filled with conflict and agony. In speaking of a Jewish Hasidic Master, Elie Wiesel says something similar: "The beauty of Rebbe Barukh [of Medzebozh] is that he could speak of faith not as opposed to anguish but as being part of it. 'Faith and the abyss are next to one another,' he told his disciple. 'I would even say: one within the other. True faith lies beyond questions; true faith comes after it has been challenged.'"[14] Can you resonate with this? What have been the greatest trials in your life? Those tribulations are when our faith is exposed— and trained. The writer to the Hebrews says it like this: "No discipline seems enjoyable at the time,* but painful. Later on, however, it yields the peaceful fruit of righteousness to those who have been trained by it" (Heb. 12:11). Our faith goes through training in the hard times. Real-life training. Disappointments and losses in life can disorient us. They cause us to ask what is real. Things are often not as they seem.

The invitation is real, but the woman, being beckoned to come, beckoned to speak, is aware of these threats to their love. There are foxes in the church. They want to spoil the beauty. We can look at this in both a corporate and individual way.

FOXES IN THE CHURCH

Let's start with the corporate. St. Augustine identifies the foxes as heretics in the church (vineyard). Cunningly, they stoke division in the church to steal the bride away. Augustine points to another part of the Old Testament where foxes destroyed a vineyard: Judges 15:3–5. This passage is one of the echoes I was referring to in the previous section. Read together, these verses help us. One of our greatest teachers

---

* Profound understatement!

in the church read Scripture this way. And it is quite a story that unfolds through chapters 14 and 15 of Judges. You can read for yourself the riddle Samson wages with the Philistines during his marriage to a young Philistine woman and how his wife was then given to a man accompanying him without his knowledge. Augustine sees this as a picture of heretics taking Christ's bride, "attempt[ing] to drag the Church, Christ's body, into their own camp."[15]

Samson's reaction is hard to stomach. He catches three hundred foxes, pairs them up by their tails, lights a torch between the tails of each pair, and scatters them out to burn havoc over the Philistines' grain, vineyards, and olive groves (Judges 15:3–5). Augustine sees a picture here that the foxes must be caught and refuted so "they do not lay waste the vineyard, the Church." He sees the significance of the foxes' tails as a metaphor of the "rear ends of heretics[.] Their fronts display a deceptive charm, but their rear ends are bound, that is sentenced, and they drag firebrands behind them, to burn up the fruits and works of those seduced by them. . . . It is the way the foxes look from the front that those they have seduced see; and what comes behind that is fire."[16]

The woman in the Song speaks for the vulnerability of the church. We can get caught up in the signs of spring and get manipulated by the foxes. False teachers are certainly in that category. Still today, we see how rampant they are. The fire that they bring behind their tails is so destructive!

But sometimes their charming front display is even more deceptive. They may seem to confess an orthodox theology and to be doing important, "good" work for the church, but manipulative and abusive behavior tells a different story about their faith. These foxes are more difficult to catch. And they may be more destructive because those who have been led by them and then suffered the effects of their abuse now associate the foxes *with* the church. I can identify with the woman in the Song, saying, *Do you see the foxes? I can't come out of the clefts of the rock quite yet. I'm too vulnerable.* So many victims of abuse in the church, particularly women, are not believed when they come forward. Instead of receiving the help and care they need, they are often shamed for seeking it because the foxes have assimilated into the vineyard. They look like grape-tenders or gatekeepers. This is why we need to bring this to the Bridegroom who knows his sheep. *Help us catch the foxes, Lord. You know they are there, coming after your bride, your church, your vineyard.* I take comfort in these words from the woman. Real life can rock our faith sometimes. But God wants to hear about it. He wants us to call out to him. He sees. That is real life too. When you're going through winter, spring doesn't seem real anymore. But it is. Sunday is coming. And all the foxes will be exposed and caught.

THE FOXES IN OUR OWN SOULS

This challenge can apply to each individual in the church as well. The foxes can serve as a metaphor for the sin, disillusionment, and doubt that want to disintegrate our faith. Do we see them, or are we ignoring them? God may be calling us out because we have turned inward. Our love for him has dulled. Maybe we are going through the motions, praying on occasion, getting to church, and trying to live a moral life, but our hearts are somewhere else. We aren't listening and looking (Song 2:8). We aren't attentive to his Spirit or his people. We are living our own lives with Christianity sprinkled in. We are not living the faith we confess. We can't seem to mesh the world of the habitual self[17]—who goes to work, the grocery store, schleps the children around, keeps the house clean, laundry done, maybe can stay awake for a movie before bed, only to wake up the next morning and repeat—with the world that we sing, hear, and talk about on Sunday mornings. They seem so disconnected.

Maybe there is a pattern of sin that you just can't free yourself from. You never thought you'd still be dealing with this now. Instead of spiritual maturation, you have merely become better at masking it, maybe even to yourself. Sin is like the destructive foxes with firebrands on their tails. It pairs up with other sin and sets off through the vineyard. It won't stop there, as it moves to the grains and the olive groves. From the front, you look like you've got everything under control, but then everything burns down and leaves you destitute.

Then there's disillusionment. Christianity turns out not to be the happy blueprint you thought it was: I live this kind of life, hang out with these kinds of people, make these "good" decisions, and God will bless me with a great life that blesses others. You've lost the joy. You've lost the plot. Those you looked up to are not who they presented themselves as. Church leaders fall into moral failure. Your parents get divorced. Your spouse leaves you for another lover. You never find your soulmate. Your kids grow to have minds of their own. You find out that the easy answers you thought you had about justice, life, wealth, and mercy are more complicated and nuanced. It turns out you aren't changing the world for Christ like you thought. Maybe you find that there is a lot you need to unlearn. Perhaps you've lost sight of the meaningfulness in faith. Your new questions can't be satisfied with an apologetics lesson. And the famous, go-to Christian celebrity apologist turned out to be a sexual predator.[18] You or someone you love may get a life-altering illness. What if you lose someone you love? What if it's a child? How can we bear these burdens and tragedies and also know God's goodness and faithfulness? How can we begin to hope, imagine, and see beauty again?

There are a lot of foxes. I'm so glad the bride articulates this for us. Now we can say it too.

If you continue to read the Song, including the next line, you will see that the woman's faith is assured of the spring invitation that she received.

RISING FROM AFFLICTION

Elie Wiesel spoke of faith and anguish being intertwined, quoting Rebbe Barukh [of Medzebozh]: "Faith and the abyss are next to one another . . . one within the other." Faith is called forth in anguish. Anguish is where we learn of faith's substance. Have we been holding onto appearances? Having the "right" doctrine, living the "Christian" life? Who is your Jesus? What causes does he support? Which communities does he get behind? Or, to summarize Christopher Ash regarding the big question in Job, how does God treat the people he loves?[19]

Why do we have to anguish? The woman in the Song tells us that she is lovesick (Song 2:5). And that's it, right? Let's listen to her. The substance of faith is Christ himself, where our affections are and our trust rests. The abyss helps reveal our false hopes. In that darkness we find our deepest longings and groanings—our real hope and expectation—and develop the trust that Christ gives himself to us. He is present with us. The challenge of the abyss reveals what we love.

Don't get me wrong, doctrine and obedience are important. But if they forgo the substance of Christ himself and his love, we are merely confessing and acting upon the *appearance* of truth and sanctification. They are foxes with firebrands if they are not filled with Christ's presence. Do we really believe, down to our bones, what we say? Or is it an illusion? Do we crumble when we are deprived of what we are seeking? What are we toiling for?* What do our good works get us?

Part of the sickness and ache of human love is the vulnerability in it. God seems to be slipping out of the woman's grasp over and over again in the Song. We see a theme of presence and absence. And we must wrestle with her on the question of divine presence in our lives: *Does God show up for us? Can we really be comforted by him when he seems so transcendent? Are his promises real?* Many of us know the ache of the absence of a loved one. How can we take the anguish of an absent God? It's as if he is here, but he isn't. The very framework of the Song highlights this point. We don't see God in a narrative or hear

---

* Ecclesiastes, anyone?

about him in didactic teaching. He is in the allegory. He is in the poetry, in the song, even in her dreams. And like a dream, the scenes keep shifting faster than we can process them. As Old Testament scholar Chloe Sun says about what we learn in the Song, "God's presence does not conform to human expectations or even to his own norms of presence."[20]

It just doesn't. We know how *we* want him to be present. We want light from darkness. We want the morning to break through the shadows. We want Christ to take our pain away and fix our problems. We want his church to be a place of goodness. And we certainly don't want to be wavering in our faith, finding that the crust of our faith has a hollow middle. We still see the darkness of night until the day breaks. Our troubles can be like mountains that divide us from Christ.[*] How can we get to him?

We can't.

The Song reveals that God comes to her—to us—reminding her of his presence.

> Listen! My love is approaching.
> Look! Here he comes,
> leaping over the mountains,
> bounding over the hills.
> My love is like a gazelle
> or a young stag. (Song 2:8–9a)

He then reminds her of the reality of his promises, inviting her into that life, beckoning her voice and participation in it

---

[*] Like the mountains he is leaping over in Song 2:9 to get to her.

(Song 2:10–14). We get something of a wedding vow from the woman right after bringing the foxes before him. She echoes the covenant promise that God reverberates throughout Scripture. She knows the spousal love of God.[21]

My love is mine and I am his;
he feeds among the lilies. (Song 2:16)

The bride-to-be has a new confidence. She has hope with substance. She is good with her vulnerability. So with his proposal, she begins to come out of the crevices of the cliff and remembers that the young stag who came barreling over the mountains and hills to get to her is with her as she perseveres to the big day. The scene ends with her faith in the promise:

Until the day breaks
and the shadows flee,
turn around, my love, and be like a gazelle
or a young stag on the divided mountains. (Song 2:17)

By repeating *gazelle, young stag, my love,* and *mountains,* she revitalizes her alert to listen and look (2:8–9). Spring is here, but day is still breaking. We can acknowledge and face the shadows because even if we can't see it yet, we are taking root in God's presence. This is soul-shaping business. But rest assured, he's approaching, coming, leaping, bounding, standing, gazing, peering, and, more intimately, feeding among the lilies.[22] He is preparing us, revealing the substance of our faith, as we get ready to metaphorically walk the aisle.

Nineteenth-century pastor Charles Spurgeon preached

that this verse is the one most frequently on his heart as the darkness in the world lays heavy on him.[23] If one of the world's most beloved Baptist pastors can admit to the darkness he feels, maybe we can too. And maybe we can really be present when our brothers and sisters in the faith are experiencing it. How do we do that? We become partners in affliction. We listen and look. We stay in the room, as witness to their stories, holding them together. We don't make them feel less of a Christian because their faith is being challenged. We don't downplay the darkness they are in. We see and name the foxes with them. We sit with them. We lament with them. We don't try to fix them. And for goodness' sake, we don't fill their ears with "shoulds." A friend once consoled me as I was talking about something I should do better by telling me that "*should* is an asshole." This line will probably be edited out because Christian authors shouldn't say *asshole*. But my friend's coarse phrase has helped me so much. Shame will never get us out of the crevices of the cliff (Song 2:14). Shame is part of the shadows. We need the invitation to listen and look for the signs of spring, the day breaking, our spouse coming for us. We need help from others to see what's real—that Christ wants to see our lovely face and hear our sweet voice. To show us that although we may see deadness and feel the effects of pruning, our roots are growing. Spring is coming. And "until the day breaks and the shadows flee," we need to help one another petition Christ, as the woman does, to turn around. That's what we can give each other. And in that, our withness is a participation in Christ's presence with them through it.

And a funny thing happens. Those mountains that we thought were dividing us from Christ's love, that made him seem so far off, weren't what we thought they were. Things are not as they seem. He's been nearby all along. Just as she uses his vows speaking of her belonging in Song 2:17, he uses her very words that we see in Song 2:18 on their wedding day. After praising her beauty from head to toe, he says, "Until the day breaks and the shadows flee, I will make my way to the mountain of myrrh and the hill of frankincense" (Song 4:6). He uses temple language to describe her body; she is rooted in his presence. She *is* the mountain and the hill. The temple mountain of Jerusalem—that's us! The expectation has built to its climax, and they will consummate their love, Christ and his church-bride.

QUESTIONS FOR PERSONAL REFLECTION AND GROUP DISCUSSION

1. How do you see Christianity right now, both in America and across the globe? How has the church helped or hindered you to make sense of the world?

2. What is your relationship with the church like? Have you faced disillusionment with the church or maybe even God? How have you or are you working through that? Who have you been able to share this story with? Here are some guiding questions to help in answering:[24] How have your relationships in the church changed over time? How did people react when you reached out for help? Do you have any specific memories you can share that impacted you? How have your experiences affected your feelings about

church? About God? What do you hope for the future of the church? Do you think your expectations may change? How would you hope for others in the church to be impacted by you over time?

3. How would you name the "foxes in the vineyard," areas that may have a deceptive charm behind a nice front display, in these categories for the church:
   - false teaching
   - institutional systems
   - bad character and spiritual maturity
   - personal sin, disillusionment, and doubt

4. How do you want God to answer these deceptive charms that you've revealed in answering question 3? What may he be revealing by not answering in that way? How could you imagine seeing Christ in others at this time? How can you be Christ to others now?

NOTES

1. Mike Bird, "Is Evangelical Worship like Going to a Coldplay Concert with a TED Talk?," *Word from the Bird* (substack), May 27, 2022, https://michaelfbird.substack.com/p/is-evangelical-worship-like-going.
2. Susan Friend Harding, "Representing Fundamentalism: The Problem of the Repugnant Cultural Other," *Social Research* 58, no. 2 (Summer 1991): 373–93.
3. See Kristin Kobes Du Mez, *Jesus and John Wayne* (New York: Liveright, 2020).
4. See Curt Thompson, *The Soul of Desire: Discovering the Neuroscience of Longing, Beauty, and Community* (Downers Grove, IL: InterVarsity Press, 2021).
5. D. C. Schindler, *Love and the Postmodern Predicament: Rediscovering the Real in Beauty, Goodness, and Truth* (Eugene, OR: Cascade, 2018), 128.
6. Schindler, *Love*, 137.
7. See Adam Young, "Why Your Story Makes It Hard To Hope," *The Place We Find Ourselves* (podcast), season 1, episode 18, August 6, 2018, https://theplacewefindourselves.libsyn.com/18-why-your-story-makes-it-hard-to-hope.
8. "The terms 'terror,' 'terrible,' and 'terrific,' Chambers tells us, are rooted in the Indo-European base *ters-* / *tres-* (to shake)." See Patricia T. O'Conner and Stewart Kellerman, "How Terror Gave us Terrific," Grammarphobia, August 1, 2013, https://www.grammarphobia.com/blog/2013/08/terror-terrific.html.
9. Hans Kvalbein, "Go Therefore and Make Disciples . . . : The Concept of Discipleship in the New Testament," *Themelios* 13, no. 2 (January 1988), https://www.thegospelcoalition.org/themelios/article/go-therefore-and-make-disciples-the-concept-of-discipleship-in-the-new-testament/.
10. Kvalbein, "Go Therefore."
11. For links to my documentation of the public part of this process see, Aimee Byrd, "Leaving the OPC," *Aimee Byrd* (blog), October 22, 2021, https://aimeebyrd.com/2021/10/22/leaving-the-opc/.
12. One example: "Let us then come within the holy of holies, that is, the Song of Songs. For we are taught by this superlative form of expression that there is a superabundant concentration of holiness within the holy of holies, and in the same way the exalted Word promises to teach us mysteries of mysteries by the agency of the Song of Songs." In Gregory of Nyssa, *Gregory of Nyssa: Homilies on the Song of Songs*, trans. Richard A. Norris Jr., ed. Brian E. Daley and John T. Fitzgerald (Atlanta: Society of Biblical Literature, 2012), 29.
13. "My love calls to me: Arise, my darling. Come away, my beautiful one. For now the winter is past; the rain has ended and gone away. The blossoms

appear in the countryside. The time of singing has come, and the turtle-dove's cooing is heard in our land. The fig tree ripens its figs; the blossoming vines give off their fragrance. Arise, my darling. Come away, my beautiful one. My dove, in the clefts of the rock, in the crevices of the cliff, let me see your face, let me hear your voice; for your voice is sweet, and your face is lovely" (Song 2:10–14).

14. Elie Wiesel, *Four Hasidic Masters and Their Struggle against Melancholy*, (Notre Dame, IN: University of Notre Dame Press, 1978), 59.
15. Augustine, *The Song of Songs: Interpreted by Early Christian and Medieval Commentators*, trans. and ed. Richard A. Norris Jr., *The Church's Bible* (Grand Rapids: Eerdmans, 2019), 129.
16. Augustine, *Song*, 129.
17. I am borrowing this term from John Keats.
18. Daniel Silliman and Kate Shellnut, "Ravi Zacharias Hid Hundreds of Pictures of Women, Abuse During Massages, and a Rape Allegation," *Christianity Today*, February 11, 2021, https://www.christianitytoday.com/news/2021/february/ravi-zacharias-rzim-investigation-sexual-abuse-sexting-rape.html.
19. "The book of Job is not about suffering in general, and certainly not about sufferings common to men and women the world over. Rather it is about how God treats his friends." Christopher Ash, *Job: The Wisdom of the Cross*, Preaching the Word, ed. R. Kent Hughes (Wheaton, IL: Crossway, 2014), 42–43.
20. Chloe T. Sun, *Conspicuous in His Absence: Studies in the Song of Songs and Esther* (Downers Grove, IL: IVP Academic, 2021), 80.
21. For more on this, see Aimee Byrd, *The Sexual Reformation: Restoring the Dignity and Personhood of Man and Woman* (Grand Rapids: Zondervan Reflective, 2022), 90–94.
22. We will unpack how the lilies represent Christ's people in chapter 6.
23. Charles Haddon Spurgeon, "Darkness Before the Dawn (SS2:17)," in *Charles Spurgeon on the Song of Solomon: 64 Sermons to Ignite a Passion for Jesus! Christian Classics Treasury* (2013), Kindle, 337.
24. Borrowed and adapted some of these questions from the Adult Attachment Interview in Daniel Siegel, *Mindsight: The New Science of Personal Transformation* (New York: Bantam, 2011), 173.

BOATLOADS
OF SHAME

Whenever the topic of shame comes up in the Byrd household, my husband belts out, "Boatloads of shame!" It's from an Avett Brothers song.[1] It's kind of funny, but mostly because it's true. Shame never feels light. I am only beginning to understand shame and its destructiveness. I'm learning why my mind and body started speaking the signs of trauma: I have been suffering from carrying boatloads of public shaming from officers in the church. It was a bit jolting to my system at first to see posts about me online like "Jezebel," "dangerous," "I wish her husband loved her enough to tell her to shut up," "satanic," and memes of transgendered women who represented me, as well as inflammatory comments about my appearance or my hair, saying my femininity looks withdrawn, and commenting that I look haggard and brutish because I am supposedly trying to foster a "kick-ass" look.[2] My first reaction in seeing the beginnings of this behavior was to try and brush them off as a few fringe haters. Except, it's especially disturbing that many of these men pastor and govern congregations. But what I saw in the beginning was only the tip of the iceberg. The first sight was the boatloads of shame heaped on me publicly. Beneath that tip is a festering theology of the nature of men and women, worldly notions of power, and a church governance that fosters it all, placing procedure over people—procedure that can be molded to benefit the men exercising it.

Surely, I believed, bringing evidence of their behavior through the proper channels of church government would bring justice and deal with these church leaders who are disqualifying themselves from office by going after a sister in Christ this way.* After all, many officers in the denomination were appalled by this behavior and ready to support me through it.[3] That list dwindled significantly as I began to document how poorly my case was being handled. As it turned out, sessions, presbyteries, and the denomination as a whole were willing to let me continue to hold the heavy, heavy shame. Three years later—after seeing and hearing things my own elders said about me behind my back, after sitting in a presbytery meeting where I was mocked and referred to as "that lady," after a presbytery committee report suggested I am as guilty as the perpetrators (that's a tactic called sin-leveling) and that my writing provoked it all, after being openly reviled as a "raging wolf" among other things during a presbytery trial, after another presbytery failed to take action when one of their pastors posted a YouTube video calling them to act

---

* And many others. I just turned into their main target.

against me (in which I was compared to a barking dog), after blogs were written about how I am the general of the feminist army, after sermons preached about God's "perfect hatred" against feminism, and after yet another presbytery meeting that failed to deal with one of the officers casting blame on me—the only apologies I have received are personal ones from some of my former elders and a few who tried to help but could not. No public apologies. Boatloads of shame. The most the denomination will call it is "error." Well, not all of it. Only the words "raging wolf." Here, hold that shame, Aimee. Many survivors of spiritual, sexual, or domestic abuse never receive apologies, never get restoration, never receive vindication. It makes one wonder: Who really is disillusioned? Those of us who peek behind the curtain, or the Great Wizards running the show?

The worst part of the boatloads isn't the verbal assault. The worst part is the lack of empathetic witness and accountability from those who can do something about it. Learning that abusers abuse because they can, because the church allows it, is like being in the middle of the ocean, trying to navigate this boatload of shame you're in, only to find out the boat is full of holes. You're going down. You realize you are not safe. And it messes with your sense of self. *Is it me? Am I this bad? How did I get in this boat? Am I not worth protection? Who is going to help me out?*

The story that shame tells is that you are not worthy. You do not belong. You do not have what it takes.[4]

Secular psychology is doing a lot of work on the way shame disintegrates us, neurobiologically and interpersonally.[5] But maybe the church needs to take a good look at this too as we ask what is behind her underlying and pervasive theology of power. Why do we see so little repentance in the church when stories of hatred, cover-up, and abuse surface? Isn't the invitation of the gospel one of finding freedom and reconciliation in repentance? What kind of hope are we left with when we refuse to look at the wounds and face the darkness? What kind of hope can the church offer if her leaders will not care for her wounds and will not reveal their complicity? What kind of Christ do they preach when they won't move toward true reconciliation with his people? Shame chokes out our hope, making us feel like God doesn't care enough or that we aren't good enough. If we stuff all this down, we are only pretending. We can't develop the healing scars we need. And then we miss the good news.

CHURCH FACE

Why do so many go through the motions of church life, often falling short of *entering* and *living in* the world of new life in Christ with all our senses? Why do we struggle to be known? I gave an extreme example from my own life, but shame isn't only something we experience from others. We are pretty good at shaming ourselves. Shame tells a tale about your value. It speaks to who you are and says, "You're not good enough." Researcher and author Brené Brown says we can easily fill in the blanks when we think we don't measure up: not smart enough, not successful enough, not attractive enough, not skinny enough, not healthy enough, not spiritual enough.[6] Medical doctor Curt Thompson refers to this as the "awful narrating self"[7] or the "shame attendant."[8] And Brown calls it the gremlins in your head.[9] You know this narrator too. We all do. When we listen to these gremlins, we start feeling as if no one would like us if they really knew us. And so, like Adam and Eve after the fall, we cover up. But not only with clothes. We cover up with sanitized smiles, with advanced degrees, with nice shoes, with HGTV-worthy homes, with curated Instagram pages, with "I'm good. How are you?" (Okay, my gremlins are telling me that I just revealed my age. Should I have said TikTok?—*checks spelling for this cooler social media app and removes the space between the Tik and the Tok.* BeReal, Aimee.)

We are particularly good at covering up on Sunday mornings. My friend calls it "church face."* We all know that the gremlins can be more exacerbating on our way to church. Those coming alone battle how this is magnified in worship. The messages from their own narrating selves are compounded by a heightened sense of their aloneness among other Christians. Talk about disillusionment! How is it that our brothers and sisters in worship can make one feel so isolated? Like you don't measure up to the contemporary gospel ideal of the nuclear family?

Meanwhile, those trying to get a whole family to church on time have a different challenge. Normal things like brushing our teeth become major obstacles when we look in the mirror and discover a stain on our shirt. The children decide it's a good day to experiment with their wardrobe boundaries.

---

* Shout out to Shannan Thorhauer!

The dog is somehow running in the neighbors' yard as we are scrambling to find our car key. *Who is watching the dog?* We become highly irritable as the weight of our own inadequacies bears down. So we take it out on our spouse, of course, who can't seem to do anything right this morning. Somehow, on the ride there, we are supposed to switch into holy mode. But the best we can do is the silent treatment. We unload in the parking lot with stress and contempt until we encounter the first smiley person ready to greet us. And there it is, *church face*. We act as if we all have it together.

I'm saying "we," but maybe it's just me and my friend. Maybe you have your act together on Sunday morning. But you still probably have a bit of church face. The Sunday morning hustle is a safer example. We don't share our stories. We don't tell our secrets. We can't be vulnerable. There's the wife who walked out on her family to the surprise of everyone in church. "She was struggling? Did you know? Me neither!" There's the high school senior who is full of doubt about God. Quietly. Outwardly, she answers the questions "correctly" in Sunday School. There's the man who had a panic attack on Friday and is terrified it may happen again while trapped in worship. The person sitting next to you doesn't have job security and is afraid to ask for help. No one seems to even engage with the single woman in her late thirties. She feels so alone in God's household. Many of us do. We're all just smiling because we should be further along on the sanctification scale by now. There's that word *should* again. Shame and *should* go hand in hand. We let our awful narrating selves make us feel like imposters who don't have what it takes. We must be vulnerable to be known, and that can be terrifying. What if church is not a safe place to be known? We need to talk about the masks we wear and the silence we keep.

Thompson sees shame as a weapon evil uses since the fall to "(1) corrupt our relationships with God and each other, and (2) disintegrate any and all gifts of vocational vision and creativity."[10] It isolates and paralyzes us. There's a difference between guilt and shame. Guilt speaks to something wrong that we did. Shame speaks to our personhood, who we are. There is a place for both, but shame doesn't want us to recognize that. It works best in secret. It's a clever tactic because we so hate the feeling of shame. To try to avoid it, we hide ourselves from others and from God like Adam and Eve. Yet we long to be known, seen, gazed upon even,[11] by God himself. The very thing that we long for we run from. We long to see and feel that gaze and hear, "You are absolutely beautiful, my darling; there is no imperfection in you" (Song 4:7). It is an expression where Christ recognizes himself in his bride, like Adam, "This one, at last, is bone of my bone and flesh of my flesh" (Gen. 2:23). *At last.* We long to be looked upon and recognized this way now because our hearts long for this greater fulfillment in eternity.

BEING GAZED UPON

I n the contexts of both verses above, the woman is naked and not ashamed. That's what we want, right? We want a kind of love that sees us in our most vulnerable condition—soul-naked—and embraces us. But we struggle to believe this kind of thing is real. Being soul-naked, or physically naked even in the most godly, intimate conditions, leaves us vulnerable. We are often uncomfortable there. And we run from the gaze that we long for—before friends and family in baring our souls, before spouses in romantic intimacy, and before God. It can terrify us. So we put on the masks.

When you look at a group picture that you are in, who is the first person you zone in on? Yourself, right? *How do I look? How do others see me?* Maybe you stay at the superficial appearance, but maybe you look deeper. *What is my expression saying? What story am I telling? How am I?* There you are, captured in a moment, for the gaze of yourself and all others looking. Tension pulls between wanting to be seen and the anxiety of being seen. Sometimes we notice the mask we were wearing.

How do you want to be seen? What story do you want others to hear about your life? Maybe you haven't asked this question directly, but we are hustling to curate our story all the time in our curated social media accounts, our wardrobes, and our interactions.

Here's a similar yet deeply different question: *What do you think people see when they look at you?* What story are they telling themselves about you? This is something we cannot control. Some agonize over this, and others completely block the thought out, either choosing to believe most people accept the story they present or pretending other people don't care because thinking otherwise is too devastating to bear.

That leads to the next question: *How are you?* What's your real story? Sometimes this weighs on us when we are alone, undistracted. Do you know another time we feel it weighing down? When someone is really looking at us. You know what

I mean. Sometimes we can feel the gaze before we make eye contact. What is that sense that we have? I'm not sure how we "feel" a gaze, but most of us have. And we all know that there are boundaries with how we look at each other—I'm not merely talking about sexual propriety, but social awkwardness. Every now and then, and not in a creepy way, someone really looks at us. It can be uncomfortable. More often than not, we look away, wanting them to look away. In that moment you are feeling seen in a way that asks these very questions: How are you? What is your real story? We want it deeply, but it terrifies us.

Shame is the cause. Since the fall, "to be human is to be infected with this phenomenon we call shame," as Curt Thompson puts it.[12] So if someone is really looking at you, your thoughts might be, "You will not measure up. How could anyone possibly love you if they knew the real you?" Our adversary leverages shame to keep us alone and entrapped in sin.[13] It's so dark and ugly—how can we be involved in creating beauty? In resurrection? Some of the shame is from what others have done to us, and some is of our own doing. So many people carry shame and trauma from abuse or neglect. Shame entraps us with messages about our value and diminishes our sense of self. If the people we love knew what was going on in our minds and the things we have done or that have been done to us—the very real sin that is such a violation of beauty, truth, and goodness— they would need to look away. We can't bear the gaze that we long for because we do not see ourselves as worthy.

So we get stuck in patterns of depression, isolation, and sin. When we think of the stain of what has been done to us in abuse or neglect or what we have done to ourselves and others in sin, we struggle to see a way forward. Shame sticks to us, in a sense. How can we talk about beauty now? You can't exercise shame off with the story you are hustling; it doesn't work. Good works don't melt the shame off either. The masks we wear to cover it up might feel like they are working for a while. But the fear grows inside of us that we will be found out. We keep pointing to the masks we wear to distract from bearing the gaze into our realness. But they lose their adhesive. We can't keep it up. We try to fulfill our longings in other ways. Sometimes sinful ways. We have superficial relationships. Yet the desire to be known just won't go away.

The good news is that God comes for us. And so we need to consider Christ's bearing our shame on the cross, despising it, while the Father looked at him (Heb. 12:2). And we need to rejoice in what God sees when he beholds us now. How does this affect the way that we see, talk about, and relate to others?

Why does it seem we are more attracted to power than love? Power over our stories, power over our image, power over our own sanctification even. Can we take off our church face and be soul-naked with one another in appropriate ways? Or with ourselves? How can we have communion without shame?

DIRECTING OUR GAZE

Do not stare at me because I am dark,
For the sun has gazed on me.
My mother's sons were angry with me;
they made me take care of the vineyards.
I have not taken care of my own vineyard. (Song 1:6)

Her companions are staring at her. She senses or antici-pates their gaze. And what is the woman's first reaction? That the sun has also gazed on her, making her dark. She is vulnerable. This woman has the confidence to say it. This moment is a turning point for all whom she represents: Israel, the church, you, me. The majesty of Christ provokes her con-fession, which we know he already took to the cross. For her and for us. So we too can say we're vulnerable.

Here is another lyric in the Song of Songs that activates other parts of Scripture as we see subtle echoes. In a sense, we hear the whole story of Israel's exile echoed. In Lamentations, Jerusalem appears as a woman, Daughter Zion. Verse one begs us to look at her:

> How she sits alone,
> the city once crowded with people!
> She who was great among the nations
> has become like a widow.
> The princess among the provinces
> has been put to forced labor. (Lam. 1:1)

We read that "all the splendor has vanished from Daughter Zion" (Lam. 1:6). The whole lament is a gaze upon the dark-ness of the shame that is Jerusalem, Daughter Zion. "All who honored her now despise her, for they have seen her naked-ness. She herself groans and turns away. Her uncleanness stains her skirts" (Lam. 1:8–9). Even now women feel the shame that comes with that skirt metaphor. As John Calvin put it, "The Prophet seems to allude to menstruous women who hide their uncleanliness as much as they can; but such a thing is of no avail, as nature must have its course." In comparing this to Jerusalem, he says that their reproach was "on their skirts, because they could not hide their disgrace. For shame often makes men to hide their evils and silently to bear them, because they are unwilling to expose themselves to the mockery of their enemies."[14]

But Jesus was willing. It's almost as if the woman in the Song (shall we call her Daughter Zion too?) speaks in the knowledge that she and the Messiah are so united that her story is wrapped up in the story of Christ. Here, her mother's brothers—children of Zion, not outsiders—exploit her. Betrayal by our own spiritual siblings is the cross of both Jesus and his church. The evil of spiritual abuse can be seen throughout church history and in our own experiences today. To be exploited and abused by our mother's sons is a deep violation. She names it.

We can hear the echoes of these verses in the New Testament when the hemorrhaging woman makes her way to touch Jesus's clothes and is instantly healed (Mark 5:25–34). She suffered from bleeding for twelve years—a number that symbolizes the twelve tribes of Israel and the twelve commissioned disciples of Jesus—Israel and the church. Oh, the shame that she walked with for those twelve years, her uncleanliness literally staining her skirts! But one faithful touch of the back of the Bridegroom's clothing and she is clean! When she confesses to Jesus what she did, he says, "Daughter . . . your faith has saved you. Go in peace and be healed from your affliction" (Mark 5:34). He looks at her now—and at us, Daughter Zion, sister, bride—having washed her clean, saying, "You are all fair, my love, And there is no spot in you" (Song 4:7 NKJV). No stain, no shame, only beauty.

HOPE FACES THE DARKNESS

We're working with a lot of figures and metaphors here, so stay with me as we move from the gazing/staining/ laboring cluster and into the vineyard. The woman in the Song tells us that her brothers angrily forced her to labor in other vineyards so that she could not take care of her own. The Song is full of imagery and metaphors. These literary devices are such good teachers. They beckon our senses to participate in the emotion that they evoke. Spiritual formation isn't merely about learning the right doctrines. God's Word often appeals to and awakens our senses and invokes our imaginations in order to transform our character, to create in us a longing for him and a hope for his presence. And neurobiological science has shown that when we learn, it doesn't begin in the rational left hemisphere of our brain as we are conditioned to think in modern Western society. Fact versus feelings is a false dichotomy. We process first through our senses and emotions, using our right hemisphere.[15] God designed us this way. And we have all kinds of imagery and metaphor in the Song, like gardens, royal courts, temples, and vineyards, rousing our senses.

Consider how this passage evokes us. Although she is saying, "Don't look at me," these metaphors are powerfully directing us *to look* into the darkness of her condition. I love this. We often cheapen hope with optimism, directing our gaze away from the darkness and pretending it's not there. "All is well! Put on your smile. God is good!" How can we speak of our insecurities when we have been given so much? How can we admit that darkness is invading our very selves when we supposedly know the end of the story—when we have the gospel? It is easier to speak of the darkness *out there* than for anyone to see the darkness *in us*. Who can bear it? I feel what the woman is feeling when she speaks powerfully through this new vineyard metaphor. And the metaphors have switched for a reason. Jill Munro describes the garden imagery as "unsullied delight for the lovers, a place where they are withdrawn from the world and free of its cares." But "the vineyard is presented primarily as a valuable asset, liable to despoliation and in need of constant care and attention."[16] The woman's brothers were excellent manipulators. As they are calling her to this labor, they know what the cost will be to her. Oh, how many times do we see this story playing out in our lives? We don't want to look at it and name it. The imagery invokes my emotions of times when I have been sucked into this story of shame.

God is teaching us something about hope in his Word. In the dark places of shame, he is there. We need the courage not to downplay the ugly. We need to face it. So let's get curious and ask where else we see this imagery in Scripture. We again find a strong correlation between bride, Israel, and vineyard in Isaiah 5, the song of the vineyard. We see that the Lord planted a vineyard, expecting it to yield good grapes, but instead it yielded worthless grapes (Isa. 5:1–7). We read this song, as well as other chapters in Isaiah full of intertextual imagery with the Song of Songs, and find that these metaphors are tied so closely together: the hope of the bride is bound to the hope of the land.[17] In seeing these intertextual connections, this metaphor has grown in significance. We can practically feel the woman's shame when she confesses in the Song that she has neglected her own vineyard. Oh no! Munro notes that "it is a perfect image of the shame and rejection she feels."[18] And the woman names it. Who will cultivate her vineyard? Who will restore the land? She shows us a place where we too can face our shame. We can open our eyes in the darkness because the darkness provides more than just evidence of evil—hope can remind us *why* the darkness is evil. Because of our great worth. We know what a vineyard is supposed to be in all its glory. We know the delights that can come from it. This reveals a deep wound—shame for a vineyard in disarray. Mourn it. Hope does not deny our wounds. Hope suffers in agony, groaning for glory. The woman invites us to groan with her. More than that, she is standing before the gaze of Christ with her neglected vineyard. It's almost unbearable. But her hope tells her it is exactly what she needs.

REVERSAL OF SHAME

She was dark, a neglected vineyard. But that isn't the end of the story. Her hope is in the LORD, who says, "I will not keep silent because of Zion, and I will not keep still because of Jerusalem, until her righteousness shines like a bright light and her salvation, like a flaming torch" (Isa. 62:1). We see this reversal from darkness to radiance in the Song: "Who is this who shines like the dawn, as beautiful as the moon, bright as the sun . . . ?" (Song 6:10). Munro points out how strikingly different the Groom's language describing his bride is from the woman's description of herself at the beginning of the Song (1:6): "There, she pleads with the daughters of Jerusalem not to look at her on account of the swarthiness of her skin which the sun has caused, literally by 'looking' at her. Now, in 6.10, the woman is identified with the clarity and strength of the sun so as to draw their gaze. She who was once despised and outcast, has become their queen."[19] Munro then notes the preceding verse: "Women see her and declare her fortunate; queens and concubines also, and they sing her praises" (Song 6:9). The shame did not stick. Christ took it from her and clothed her in his radiance. His gaze makes all the difference, and now even queens sing her praises.

His gaze sees what is real. Remember that things are not as they seem. When we eventually get a picture of the "bride, the wife of the Lamb," we are taken to a "great, high mountain . . . the holy city, Jerusalem, coming down out of heaven from God, arrayed with God's glory. Her radiance was like a precious jewel, like a jasper stone, clear as crystal" (Rev. 21:10–11). Doesn't this activate our memory of this woman in the Song, who "shines like the dawn, as beautiful as the moon, bright as the sun"? And building up to that, we see the connection with the "woman clothed with the sun, with the moon under her feet and a crown of twelve stars on her head" (Rev. 12:1).* We see in this section that we must go through tribulation on our way to that Great Day. And in this revelation, we see that the bride rises! The Bible ends with the bride joining her voice with the Spirit's, beckoning all who are thirsty to come (Rev. 22:17).

How? Christ, the first to rise, is how. He's the first to love, the first to give, and the first to sacrifice. In him, we learn

---

* There's that number, twelve, again!

something profound about power. His is a wholly different kind of power in a wholly different kingdom. As theologian Hans Urs von Balthasar explains, the power we need to overcome the world and not flee from it is "the power of self-denying love."[20] This is the love of Christ. And its fruit is the opposite of shame; it is joy.

> Those who look to him are radiant with joy;
> their faces will never be ashamed. (Psalm 34:5)

THE CHURCH'S FACE

"This is my body, which is given for you."

We see these words of Jesus at the Last Supper, as he broke the bread and gave it to his disciples. Now we're back at those hard things. Who can understand them? "'Do this in remembrance of me.' In the same way, he also took the cup after supper and said, 'This cup is the new covenant in my blood, which is poured out for you'" (Luke 22:19–20).

The next thing we read about is the disciples arguing over which one of them is going to betray Christ. After that, we read: "Then a dispute arose among them about who should be considered the greatest" (v. 24). Really? Talk about "adventures in missing the point"![21] They just shared the first communion, which anticipates Christ's atonement and the great feast that awaits us in the consummation of our spousal union. "They will come from east and west, from north and south, to share the banquet in the kingdom of God" (Luke 13:29). In a sense, we should remember this every time we gather around the table, *especially* when we gather as a church family in communion.

The mystery of it all is profound. For the first fifteen hundred years of church history, communion was the center of worship, and that mystery was revered. Now we have different interpretations of how or if the elements of bread and wine (or Welch's) become Christ's body and blood and how his grace is conferred in the sacrament (or mere ordinance). In many churches, communion, or the Eucharist, is an afterthought. Some only serve it monthly. Some quarterly. In the post COVID-19 era in which we live, many are taking it from disposable prepackaged units. There is no table at all. As a result, I am becoming more and more convinced that we are missing out on the great mystery that really is the face of the church. It is a mystery, so I certainly am not going to be the one to explain it all in digestible bites.

But that is just it. We are invited not only to behold this great mystery together but also to partake in it. We are partaking in the flesh and blood of our Savior and Bridegroom. He nourishes us. He covenantally brings us into himself, saying that this is what he "fervently desire[s]" (Luke 22:15), and into communion with one another. How does that change the way we see one another? How does it change the way we treat one another?[22] We are on level ground with what we need, soul-naked before Christ and one another, and on level ground for what he gives: his body and blood. Oh, the power of this love! This is the radiant face of the church. Look how much she is loved!

She is loved because she is gift. That's why Christ does what he does. The bride/church is a gift from the Father to the

Son by the Spirit from eternity. Before the beginning of time, a covenant of redemption was made between the persons of the Godhead. This eternal covenant is intra-Trinitarian, meaning it was made between the three persons of the Father, Son, and Holy Spirit.[23] In this covenant, the Father promised to give the Son a bride, the Son promised to secure the redemption of his bride, and the Holy Spirit promised to apply his work to his people. Another mystery is that it is an election based on God's love (Eph. 2:4–5), not arbitrary or based on the merit of the bride. Our shame attendants cannot grasp this love. We are gift. The triune God loves us. God has given himself. The Son put on flesh. Do we not marvel at the incarnation as we partake in the Eucharist? And he gives his flesh and blood to his bride. He is the manna. Give us this day our daily bread. We are called into eternal communion with our Bridegroom, to join the Father in loving the Son by the Spirit.[24] This is the end to which we are headed, to which Christ spearheads and nourishes us on the way.

The collective bride of Christ gets to know something of the outgoing, overflowing love of the triune God. Jesus refers to this covenant of redemption in his High Priestly Prayer: "Father, I want those you have given me to be with me where I am, so that they will see my glory, which you have given me because you loved me before the world's foundation" (John 17:24).[25] We are given to him by the Father. We are gift. Because of the love of the Father for the Son in the Spirit.

If we do this in remembrance of him, we can see each other as gift. His power is generative: the power of self-denying love. How does that affect the way we love one another in his household? What face will outsiders see of the church in the way we love one another? Theologian Timothy Tennent also sees a corporate remembrance, that the church should "model this sacrificial and self-giving posture to the world, as we serve the poor and herald the good news of Jesus Christ to the lost."[26] Is this the face of the church? It's a face without shame that recognizes we were the lost to whom Christ came and gave himself. So we are to see our neighbors as gifts—not as projects to win over, but as people with dignity, as people to love whether they receive faith or not.

RISING FROM SHAME

Shame isolates. We keep our secrets of pain, fear, inadequacy, and sin from our senses, from our psyche, and from the gaze of others. But Christ loves us. He is preparing us for the weight of this love, and he will not have his bride covered in shame. So the very sources of our disillusionment may cause us to finally say, "I'm not okay. I am wearing masks that I didn't even realize I created. I am hustling a message that I am like everyone else, but now I see that we are all pretty lost. I'm putting expectations on others that only Christ can accomplish. I wasn't aware of how deep my needs are." Many of us are hurting. Disillusionment pressures us to ask what we really believe and who we really are.

We need to take the power from our mental gremlins telling us we are no good. If there is guilt, we need to confess it and walk in the forgiveness and freedom that Christ gives. He accepted the gift of his bride because she is given of the Father in love. Do we not accept the gift Christ gives us in love? And do we not see ourselves as the gift that we are to him? Are we allowing shame more power than it has? Oftentimes, those hurling out the shame on others can't bear the weight of the shame they carry. That's called projection. Those shaming others are so afraid they will have to look at their own shame, deal with it, or worse, bear others gazing at it that they fool themselves into thinking someone else can carry it for them. What a fool's errand!

Let's return to Psalm 34:

> Those who look to him are radiant with joy;
> their faces will never be ashamed. (Ps. 34:5)

In drawing near to Christ, we receive his light. We come out of the darkness and the isolation of shame, out of the clefts, out of the shadows. In teaching on Psalm 34, Augustine says, "We must draw near to receive his body and blood." He comments that those persecuting him "drew near to crucify him" and were "plunged into darkness," while "we are illumined by eating and drinking the Crucified."[27] These are hard things, I know. But absolutely glorious. That is our need. That is our promise.

How do we draw near to God when we feel far from him? The answer is the very thing that shame, with its counterfeit picture of glory, strives to keep from us. Shame tells us that we must attain our own glory. That was the first lie of the serpent in the beginning. See the lie for the gremlin that it is. Instead, look to Christ. Augustine reveals from this passage that the way to draw near is by repentance. Shame is deceit that keeps us from drawing close to Christ. "Think it through. If the fear of being put to shame deters you from repentance, but repentance causes you to draw near to God, do you not see that you are wearing your punishment on your face?"[28] There's your mask.

We need to despise shame because Christ does. We do this among a cloud of witnesses, those who went before us in the faith:

> Therefore, since we also have such a large cloud of witnesses surrounding us, let us lay aside every hindrance and the sin that so easily ensnares us. Let us run with endurance the race that lies before us, keeping our eyes on Jesus, the pioneer and perfecter of our faith. For the joy that lay before him, he endured the cross, despising the shame, and sat down at the right hand of the throne of God. (Heb. 12:1–2)

I could write a whole book about these verses. But in this book, I will talk more about the cloud of witnesses and the endurance with which we run.

I lay it all before you in its glory now to provide a little context as we keep our eyes on Christ and become radiant with the joy that was before him—union with his bride. For that he endured the cross, despising the shame, and now sits at the right hand of the throne of God. What a wonder! Between him and joy was the cross and shame. There he was, naked before God, mocked by those he came to die for, abandoned by many of his disciples and friends, dying the death of the worst of criminals. What kind of Messiah dies like this? Think about the gaze upon our Lord Jesus on the cross, not only by the onlookers, but by the Father himself. "Most assuredly did people see him stripped of beauty and majesty. Understandably, they shook their heads before his cross, taunting, 'Is this all that the Son of God amounts to? If he is the Son of God, let him come down from the cross'" (Matt. 27:40).[29] The people he came to serve—those he loved, those he made himself vulnerable for, those he laid down his life for—said that about him. But that is nothing compared to bearing the gaze from the Father while on the cross. How could he bear being seen by the Father while carrying our shame?

What does it mean that Jesus despised the shame? Don't you see? It's the joy. This shaming was darkness, counterfeit, *nothing* compared to the joy that awaited him: the trueness of who he is, the love of the Father by the Spirit, and the love for his bride whom he will behold. This is why the faces that look to him will never be ashamed—they are radiant with joy. The shame doesn't stick. Behold the beauty of our Savior, King, and Bridegroom!

When we get this, we begin to understand that repentance isn't about some sort of groveling about how awful we are. Repentance comes out of seeing the light in the darkness and learning more about living in light of eternity and who we are in Christ. It's the essence of the Christian life on this side of our own resurrection. Once we behold the beautiful light, shame is shown for the counterfeit that it is. Once we behold the beautiful light, we see how ugly sin is, abhor it, and want to shed it. Let's cultivate beauty here and now, looking to Christ and planting that invitation in all that we do. Artist Makoto Fujimura says that without an appreciation for beauty, culture loses its appetite for truth and goodness. He proposes that repentance itself is provoked by an encounter with the beautiful.[30] This encounter is what we desire. We want to enter into the beauty of Christ. We want others to see it radiating from us. We want to see Christ in one another, which becomes our framework for relationships and for confession. We want the world to see Christ in his church. If we are holding onto shame and guilt, we need to look to Christ. We can distinguish between the two, but the remedy is the same.

Seeing the reality of Christ leads us to repentance. Call out to the Lord for this beauty, for this joy. This isn't merely a Christian platitude; it's science. God made us to operate this way. Developments in neuroscience reveal that we are transformed by joy in our relational attachments, and this joy in love develops our sense of self and even our character.[31] Isn't it a wonder that God would have us transformed by joy? Repentance comes when we can see what is real, when we can see the shame sticking to us as the counterfeit that it is—fuzzy little critters that turned into gremlins. We will have to do this over and over, as the life of the bride in the wilderness is one of the cross on our way to glory. But what a gift repentance is for Christ's people! What freedom there is in belonging to him! In him we are able to receive him and give of ourselves in love. We gain the freedom to become what we are created for.

Maybe the reason we see so little repentance from leaders in the church is because they have missed the beauty all along. They have fallen for the counterfeit, believing that they have power over Christ's people instead of giving power to them in self-denial. They are grasping at something of no value: self-righteousness, self-protection, self-glory. Power over their image, power over their reputation, power over vulnerability. Do we want to hold onto what Christ despised?

COMMUNION WITHOUT SHAME

Here's the thing: Christianity is a confessional faith. But as necessary and beneficial as our creeds and confessions are, they can't love you. They were never meant to be alone. Theology without love is theology without God. And that's not theology at all. Theology without love is dead. We worship God in spirit and in truth. We need both. Without love, there is no beauty, no significance, and no place for our longings to land. Theology without love is not only dead; it isn't safe. And it is driven by shame. Theology without love is shameology. And you can't have communion in shame. So whether we are letting the gremlins shame and isolate us, projecting that onto others, or standing by and doing nothing while others are being shamed, it's time to see it for what it is and confess it before God and anyone we have hurt. Because Christ is better. And if you are being shamed as I was/am, we need to find a community that will help us look to Christ and see us as he does so that we can radiate his joy.

Church is where Christ's people, his bride, can delight in the Lord together. Church is where we can develop our desire together as he is preparing our souls for love. Church is where we can practice heaven, as Curt Thompson says.[32] There we find sacred siblings and advocates. There we hear, speak, and read God's Word in community. There we read the Bible with an eschatological imagination—being courted and transformed by God's Word. Church should be a safe place to ask hard questions about life, offering security in

Christ as we express our doubts, a place of protection from the harm of others, where we provoke one another to love and holiness as we gaze at Christ together. Church should offer communion without shame. Repentance comes easy in loving cultures.

Repentance comes easy in loving cultures. Yes, I said it twice. Loving cultures join Christ in despising shame. They are caught up in his joy and therefore see shame for what it is. So it is easy to confess the story shame is telling us and expose it for what it is. It is safe to confess sin in the appropriate context, to truly repent before God and to whom we have offended, and to ask what steps we can take to reconcile. After all, we are feeding on the very body and blood of our Savior together. Integrity demands that we repent in coming to the table. And if anyone in the church, especially a leader, is caught up in shaming and abuse, they will be confronted with the gospel.

We need churches that offer freedom in belonging. Biblical scholar Richard Bauckham helps us understand that "the fullest freedom is not to be found in being as free from others as possible, but in the freedom we give to each other when we belong to each other in loving relationships."[33] Belonging is freedom to give and to love. That's why I will continue to be a singer of the Song of Songs. There we find voices that show us the picture of true, uninhibited freedom in belonging exclusively to Christ. This is our telos. And if we don't have that yet in church, we can go to the "holy of holies" of Scripture for this communion while we keep showing up in his house, asking him to do his work of preparing our souls for love.

BELONGING TO A SYSTEM OR BELONGING TO CHRIST?

We may be members of a church. This membership can help us to have a united confession, clearer expectations, and submission to ecclesial government that comes with privileges and responsibilities. There is a system set in place, then, for addressing sin and abuses.

Since I'm using the word *abuse*, I want to define it. In a therapy session with an expert on the topic, I learned that spiritual abuse is when someone uses their power to do or take from another what is not rightfully theirs. As Wade Mullen defines it, "When someone treats you as an object they are willing to harm for their own benefit, abuse has occurred, and that person has become an abuser. Some of the worst forms of abuse are psychological."[34] Abuse is all about gaining and retaining power at the expense of another. It often comes in patterns. I resonate with what Mullen says about freeing yourself from abuse: "Freedom comes first by understanding, and understanding means having the language to identify and talk about your situation."[35]

Another word that needs defining is *trauma*. Peter Levine and Gabor Maté make a helpful distinction here: "Trauma is not what happens to us, but what we hold inside in the absence of empathetic witness."[36] We are left holding our stories ourselves, lacking partners and siblings in affliction.

Before being targeted by a number of its leaders, I liked my denomination. I liked that it is confessional, and I trusted in the presbyterian government. I thought I had community in my local church and confidence in the books of church order.

I believed they provided exactly that: an ordered and lawful process to protect the vulnerable. I never expected to be in the category of the vulnerable. When I began to experience the organized reviling and vicious behavior from officers in my denomination, I trusted that other church officers would confront them and call them to repentance. If it continued, I trusted that faithful undershepherds would use due process to stop the abuse and rectify the damage. Formal charges should be a last resort because we first want to informally address the heart issues, hoping for change, repentance, and reconciliation. That's what we really want. First, restoration to Christ. Second, restoration to his people.

When spiritual abuse is involved, the repentant person in spiritual authority hopefully sees that they need shepherding and are not qualified to have this kind of authority over God's people. They have so severely violated trust with God's people that a sincere apology must include appropriately sensitive action. Voluntarily stepping down would be an action that shows the weight of their responsibility to God as an office-bearer as well as setting up boundaries out of respect for the victims of their abuse. The leader should do so because the people who have been harmed, and the other people under the leader's care, are valued. It's the power of self-denying love.

That is what we would expect in Christ's church. But I've learned that those under spiritual abuse are not protected by the process. Abusers manipulate the rules to protect their power. Time and time again, those who adjudicate the process demonstrate loyalty to the denomination over the people in it. Even when there are faithful undershepherds working for righteousness. Something needs reforming, and it starts with our hearts. By the time ecclesial charges are filed, hearts have been hardened to destructive levels. But the victims of this destruction must continue to wade through the destruction to pursue justice. The i's that must be dotted and the t's that must be crossed in the formal process are but symbols and reminders of how their value has been trampled upon. The informal process can often be traumatic for the victims, as they put themselves out there with the truth only to be gaslit by the perpetrators, who attempt to manipulate others who could help, sabotage the process, and reverse the order of the victim and the offender.

While ecclesial charges may be a necessary part of the process, the process itself often hurts the very people it is ostensibly set up to protect. Charges, even if filed, victorious, and supplying a small amount of justice, are executed while the wounds of the hurting are still open, exposed, and vulnerable. Churches need to get to the root of that problem. To overcome their blind spots, church leaders need the wisdom to consult the people in the margins. The shepherds who are leading the process can gain perspective to better care for the sheep.

All denominations need to reexamine whether the systems we rely on actually work. And if they work, are they humanizing? Who pays the cost? Who is being cared for and how? What is being protected? Is the focus on the people or the process? Whose voice is magnified? How is Christ glorified? How does this affect our witness and our communion as God's people?

The effects of shame are traumatizing and disintegrating. If we want communion without shame, we need to learn how to care for the most vulnerable to it. We often need to learn from them about how to do that. We need to hear their voices. Sadly, the process to seek justice, righteousness, care, and prevent further abuse is often more traumatizing than the original offences.

We all need to learn about trauma-informed care. So I'm closing this chapter with a practical section. There are six key principles to trauma-informed care:[37]

1. **Safety:** Does the person coming forward have social support, or will she be isolated in her shame? Will she be believed or blamed? Will she be left to fend for herself? Who will advocate for her? Who will shield her from more harm?

2. **Trustworthiness and transparency:** The person coming forward for care is vulnerable. If they are coming to you for help, it is your responsibility to act in a trustworthy way.

3. **Peer support:** Rather than building more power-over structures, does your system help to equip people to care for each other? This is how we learn about one another and one-anothering.

4. **Collaboration and mutuality:** Don't keep the victim a victim. She is a gift. She has much to contribute. You need one another to grow through this. Reciprocity is key.

5. **Empowerment, voice, and choice:** These three are what is taken by sin and abuse, and these three are what needs restoring. Empowerment, voice, and choice are a basic part of what makes us human.[38]

6. **Recognize and respond to cultural, historical, and gender factors related to this trauma:** We often do not recognize our own biases and privileges and how that affects the

one harmed. We can only see from our own perspectives, so to understand the cultural, historical, and gender-related factors of this trauma, you need the help of brothers and sisters with experiences and viewpoints different than your own.

These six points originate from a resource from the Centers for Disease Control and Prevention and have been expanded a bit. Seeing this teaching so widely in print made me emotional, as each one speaks to the failures I saw. Eventually, as concerned church officers learned more about this care, some did offer it at a more personal level. But so many denominations' church order works against these very principles. Pastors and elders desperately need training in trauma-informed care and to be held accountable to implement it. The process—proper channels—needs reform to do the same. Because ultimately, we do not belong to a system, or even a church; we belong to Christ. By his common grace, the church can learn from professionals in caring for traumatized people. Because traumatized people certainly walk through their doors.

PARTNERS IN AFFLICTION

Many of you are reading this book because you have been through affliction and disillusionment in the church. I hope that by sharing some of my own story, you can better narrate your own and make connections. I hope you have trusted friends to share your stories with and to work through the shame that entangles them. That is part of what church should be—a community where we hold our testimonies together. Curt Thompson says that we need to gaze at our trauma, our grief, and our shame. We do this by "listening to each other's stories in all their interpersonal, neurobiological weight in light of the resurrection and presence of the Holy Trinity," and in this we "make way for beauty to be imagined and created."[39] The affliction is real. And it sucks. All God's people go through affliction. We are called as disciples to be partners in it. We are not alone. Gazing at our own affliction, and our brothers' and sisters' afflictions, we hold all our broken pieces up and see our fears, our inadequacies, our wounds, and our sin. It is terrifying work. But as Christ's gaze is on us, and we direct our eyes to him, something amazing begins to happen. We put ourselves in the path of beauty. And that is what we turn to next.

QUESTIONS FOR PERSONAL REFLECTION AND GROUP DISCUSSION

1. Let's answer some of the questions proposed in this chapter. How do you want to be seen? What story do you want others to hear about your life? Why do you think this version of yourself is important to you? In what ways do you think you are hustling this story? Is this story trying to mask something?

2. What do you think people see when they look at you? What story do you think they are telling themselves about you? What are the gremlins in your head saying here?
3. Swap stories with some friends or the people in your book study group. They can share the stories they tell themselves about you, and you can share the stories you tell yourself about them. How do you think your friend would answer the list of questions that follow? Use their answers as a guide to help you tell your stories:
   - What brings me joy?
   - What brings me grief?
   - What do I love?
   - Who are my people?
   - What do I really want/desire in life?
   - What do I value?
   - What are my gifts and talents?
   - What are my contributions?
   - What are my challenges?
4. Do you feel seen or known by these stories? How do they help you tell your story more truly? How do your answers to question 1 and question 2 measure up to the story swap results? What if you don't have power over your image and reputation? What are you left with? How may these exercises help you begin to learn more of the story that God is telling about you?
5. How can you help others hold their stories? How can you grow in becoming a partner in affliction? Are you a person who is safe for others to drop their church face and be vulnerable with?

NOTES

1. The Avett Brothers, "Shame," written and produced by Seth Avett and Scott Avett, *Emotionalism*, Ramseur Records, May 15, 2007.

2. See Aimee Byrd, "Genevan Commons and the Qualifications for Church Office," *Aimee Byrd* (blog), June 19, 2020, https://aimeebyrd.com/2020/06/19/genevan-commons-and-the-qualifications-for-church-office/.

3. See Aimee Byrd, "An Open Letter From Concerned Ministers and Elders in the OPC," *Aimee Byrd* (blog), June 22, 2020, https://aimeebyrd.com/2020/06/22/an-open-letter-from-concerned-ministers-and-elders-in-the-opc/.

4. Jim Wilder teaches another aspect of shame, which is healthy in spiritual growth. It is an ability to experience and process shame relationally through *hesed* love attachments. "Toxic shame communicates the message 'you are bad' . . . Healthy shame is a nonverbal spontaneous reaction to a face that is not happy to be with me. . . . We can learn to be relational in shame, so healthy shame does not leave me alone. A healthy shame message is in the form, 'I love you but believe that you stopped acting like yourself. Let me remind you how we act in this situation.'" Jim Wilder and Michel Hendricks, *The Other Half of Church: Christian Community, Brain Science, and Overcoming Spiritual Stagnation* (Chicago, IL: Moody, 2020), 131–32.

5. "Shame has a tendency to disrupt this process of 'regulating the flow of energy and information' by effectively disconnecting various functions of the mind from one another, leaving each domain of the mind as cut off from one another as we feel ourselves to be disconnected from other people." Curt Thompson, *The Soul of Shame: Retelling the Stories We Believe about Ourselves* (Downers Grove, IL: InterVarsity Press, 2015), 40.

6. See Brené Brown, *Daring Greatly: How the Courage to Be Vulnerable Transforms the Way We Live, Love, Parent, and Lead* (New York: Gotham, 2012), 25.

7. Thompson, *Soul of Shame*, 58.

8. Thompson, *Soul of Shame*, 93.

9. Brown, *Daring Greatly*, 66.

10. Thompson, *Soul of Shame*, 13.

11. See Curt Thompson, *The Soul of Desire: Discovering the Neuroscience of Longing, Beauty, and Community* (Downers Grove, IL: InterVarsity Press, 2021), 157–74.

12. Curt Thompson, M.D., *The Soul of Shame: Retelling the Stories We Believe About Ourselves* (Downers Grove, IL: IVP Books, 2015), 21.

13. Thompson, *Soul of Shame*, 22.

14. John Calvin, *Commentary on Jeremiah 48–52, Lamentations, Ezekiel 1–12*, trans. William Pringle, Calvin's Commentaries, vol. 11 (Grand Rapids: Baker, 2003), 320.

15. See Daniel J. Siegel, *Mindsight: The New Science of Personal Transformation* (New York: Bantam, 2011), 107–9; Thompson, *The Soul of Desire*, 34–53.

16. Jill M. Munro, *Spikenard and Saffron: A Study in the Poetic Language of the Song of Songs* (Sheffield: Sheffield Academic Press, 1995), 98–99.

17. See Aimee Byrd, *The Sexual Reformation*, (Grand Rapids: Zondervan Reflective, 2022).

18. Munro, *Spikenard*, 99.

19. Munro, *Spikenard*, 39.

20. Hans Urs von Balthasar, *Explorations in Theology*, vol. 2, *Spouse of the Word* (San Francisco: Ignatius, 1991), 33.

21. This was such a clever book title by Brian McLaren and Tony Campolo, *Adventures in Missing the Point: How the Culture Controlled Church Neutered the Gospel* (Grand Rapids: Zondervan, 2003).

22. For a thought-provoking talk on this see Francis Chan, "The Blood and the Bread," *Theology in the Raw*, episode 1001, https://theologyintheraw.com /podcast/1001-the-blood-and-the-bread-francis-chan/.

23. This does not signify three distinct wills in the Trinity but rather distinct personal applications and acts of the one divine will. See Scott R. Swain, "Covenant of Redemption," in *Christian Dogmatics: Reformed Theology for the Church Catholic*, ed. Michael Allen and Scott R. Swain (Grand Rapids: Baker Academic, 2016).

24. See Kelly M. Kapic, "Anthropology," in *Christian Dogmatics*, ed. Allen and Swain, 166.

25. See also Ps. 110; Rom. 8:34; Heb. 7:25; 9:24; 1 John 2:1.

26. Timothy C. Tennent, *For the Body: Recovering a Theology of Gender, Sexuality, and the Human Body* (Grand Rapids: Zondervan Reflective, 2020), 57.

27. St. Augustine, *Expositions of the Psalms*, vol. 2, translation and notes by Maria Boulding, OSB, ed. John E. Rotelle, OSA (Hyde Park, NY: New City, 2000), 31.

28. Augustine, *Psalms*, 2:32.

29. St. Augustine, *Expositions of the Psalms: 99–120*, trans. Maria Boulding, ed. Boniface Ramsey (Hyde Park, NY: New City, 2004), 112.

30. See Makoto Fujimura, *Culture Care* (Downers Grove, IL: InterVarsity Press, 2017), 49, 54.

31. See Jim Wilder, *Renovated: God, Dallas Willard, and the Church That Transforms* (Colorado Springs: NavPress, 2020), 76–77.

32. Thompson, *Soul of Desire*, 211.

33. See Richard Bauckham, *God and the Crisis of Freedom: Biblical and Contemporary Perspectives* (Louisville: Westminster John Knox, 2002), 18.

34. Wade Mullen, *Something's Not Right: Decoding the Hidden Tactics of Abuse and Freeing Yourself from Its Power* (Carol Stream, IL: Tyndale Momentum, 2020), 2.

35. Mullen, *Something's Not Right*, 4.
36. Gabor Maté, forward to *In an Unspoken Voice*, by Peter Levine (Berkeley: North Atlantic, 2010), loc. 153, Kindle.
37. See "Infographic: 6 Guiding Principles To A Trauma-Informed Approach," Center for Preparedness and Response, CDC, https://www.cdc.gov/cpr /infographics/6_principles_trauma_info.htm.
38. See Diane Langberg, *Redeeming Power: Understanding Authority and Abuse in the Church* (Grand Rapids: Brazos, 2020), 3.
39. Thompson, *The Soul of Desire*, 174.

PART 2

PARTNERS IN KINGDOM

3

HOLDING ONTO
WHAT MATTERS

What if instead of asking "How are you?" we began by asking, "What is your story?" Not to everyone we make eye contact with and share a smile. Not as a general greeting. But what if we really wanted to *know* our friends and our acquaintances in the church better?

One thing that I appreciate about Baptists is their eagerness to ask for and share testimonies. It's sometimes incorporated into their worship services. Earlier, I mentioned my leeriness of personal sharing, worried that it would become too self-centered rather than God-centered. And that is a danger. But we are designed to be storied people, and our testimonies are personal stories of how God interrupts our lives, in a sense, with the truth of who he is. Over and over again. I was asked to share my testimony at a women's conference once. They wanted that to be my whole Friday evening session: forty-five minutes of testimony. The three sessions on the topic I came to do wouldn't be shared until the next day. Their plan made me uncomfortable. Wanting to be taken seriously for the content of my work and the message and passion to share it, I didn't want to be one of those women who came and talked about herself and her personal junk for a whole session. I carried a perpetual wariness of falling into that typical froofy women's Christian ghetto where everyone talks about their feelings without a hint of theological depth. Do male speakers get asked to do this? I accepted because the women in charge of hosting were excited about the theological depth of my message. That's why they invited me. And they explained that it would be good for the listeners to get to know me so that they would be even more eager to hear the message I had to share.

I spent significant time planning those three Saturday talks, editing them over and over, and trying to get them polished for a good communication. The testimony planning was left for the plane ride. Unlike the manuscripts for my three talks, my testimony was just an outline of bullet points. The bullet points were three trials in my life. These were turning points in my story where I was faced with the question, *Who am I?*: at ten years old, with my dad's near-death car accident and that summer he spent fighting for his life; at twelve years old, with my diagnosis of scoliosis and subsequent wearing of a back brace for three and a half years; and around sixteen years old, when my parents divorced. Each of these disruptions messed with my sense of self and what I thought about God. How much is helpful to share? I was unsure how to land the whole plane of my testimony when the actual plane landed. Whatever you do, Aimee, don't have it sound cliché: "and then Jesus changed everything . . ."

After a lovely guided tour around New Braunfels and the Gruene historic district in Texas, my hosts sent me to the guest house accommodations stocked with goodies. There was wine. That's what I needed to calm my nerves for this whole testimony thing. And that glass of wine helped me think of the ending—of the talk, that is. My testimony is still being written. You see, these events revealed some things about myself. Especially the divorce. My faith was transactional. After handling the first two trials with a "strong faith," God owed me more than a broken home. And when my prayers weren't answered in the way I wanted . . . well, I've already shared some of that with you.

Turns out, sharing my testimony really did help prepare the women to hear my message the following day, but in a different way than I expected. The cool thing about it was having to carefully think about my story. I was both getting to know myself and seeing God's work in fresh ways. By narrating my story in front of all these people, I was more vulnerable than in my usual public engagements. We all held my story together. I was known by a cloud of witnesses. During the social time afterwards, these women shared personal connections, and we saw how our stories interwove. I wasn't just a speaker coming with a message anymore; I was a real person with a history and a fighting faith. Sharing my story wasn't merely sharing a message. I was sharing myself.

We are storied people, all of us. And we need to be more curious about our stories and those of others. They matter. We particularly need to be curious about the parts where God disrupts our stories. What story do you tell yourself about who you are, your journey, your desires, your disappointments, your loves, and how it all fits together?

Recognizing how our stories shape us will help us to learn better, love better, and heal better. The thing about stories is they require more than one character. We think we alone hold all this in our brains, but as author Bessel van der Kolk put it, the body keeps the score.[1] Our brains do not hold our stories individually and keep everything in a pleasant, isolated cerebral sphere inside our skulls. Our bodies *feel* our stories. They also must process them. Our health is affected by how integrated we are in doing this.[2]

The whole body of Christ keeps the score of the church's health as well.[3] Perhaps this is what Paul is referring to when he says, "For whoever eats and drinks without recognizing the body, eats and drinks judgment on himself," in addressing the Corinthians' abuses during communion (1 Cor. 11:29). How can we covenantally participate in communion with the body and blood of Christ while at the same time neglecting parts of his church body?

One distinction we need to make here is that the brain and the mind are not the same.[4] It's fascinating to learn about the mind, and so mysterious. It gets even trickier when we talk about how the mind, soul, and affections of our hearts interrelate and how they relate to the minds, souls, and affections of others. This interrelation within us happens in the context of the story that we are constantly telling ourselves and each other, both verbally and nonverbally. Faith involves so much more than our brains. Doctrine is important, but it unfolds in stories. We can't rip doctrine out to stand on its own. It was never meant to.

Doctrine is important to me because I want to know God truly. I'm not downplaying its value. But my experiences over the last three years have revealed to me the dangers of thinking of the faith in exclusively cerebral terms. Faith is gloriously more than the "right" things to believe about God. It's so easy to get caught up in a transactional mode in talking about our need for salvation and sanctification. We assent to these truths and conform to these behaviors in exchange for eternal life with God and belonging in the faith. We can easily reduce our faith to decisions and performance. We call it "submission" so it sounds more spiritual. But we shouldn't merely submit or subscribe to words about God; we need to walk in the reality of who he is and the life he gives us together.

God is inviting us to commune with him. He's preparing us for love. Theology without love—and all that holistically encompasses—is a theology of a different god. And love isn't something merely didactically taught. It's something we need to be prepared for. We learn of it through stories. And in our unmasked faces.

God isn't only after our brains. He's beckoning all our senses as embodied people, igniting our imaginations and sense of wonder, connecting our confession of who he is with the cloud of witnesses that have gone before us, and teaching us about his gift of true freedom in belonging.

OUR MINDS NEED STORY

These truths have been reinforced by my friendships and through learning. It fascinates me how the advances of science are revealing how amazing the mind is—and so vastly different from the computer model that our minds have been characterized as. As it turns out, our senses and emotions fuel the whole enterprise. Thinking doesn't merely happen inside our skulls, inside our brains. Our brains and our minds are not the same thing. Our minds need "extra-neural resources." One fascinating read about this is Annie Murphy Paul's *The Extended Mind: The Power of Thinking outside the Brain.* She postulates,

> As it is, we use our brains entirely too much—to the detriment of our ability to think intelligently. What we need to do is think outside the brain.
>
> Thinking outside the brain means skillfully engaging entities external to our heads—the feelings and movements of our bodies, the physical spaces in which we learn and work, and the minds of other people around us—drawing them into our mental processes. By reaching beyond the brain to recruit these "extra-neural" resources, we are able to focus more intently, comprehend more deeply, and create more imaginatively—to entertain ideas that would be literally unthinkable by the brain alone.[5]

In other words, we need story. And our minds, which are the narrating self, need a setting, a cast of characters, plot, point of view, and even conflict and resolution. "The literature on the extended mind suggests" our intelligence and expertise correlates to our "learning how best to marshal and apply extra-neural resources to the tasks before them."[6] We think better, smarter, when we are attuning to our senses, environment, and the minds of others.

Daniel Siegel, who first introduced us to the expression

"interpersonal neurobiology," calls it "the neurobiology of we."[7] Our minds were designed to interact with other people's minds. We cannot "know" ourselves without the witness and story we sense others sharing with us. And that is just it. We all want to be known, to be seen, and to be loved. As Curt Thompson shares in *The Soul of Desire*, "We need others to bear witness to our deepest longings, our greatest joys, our most painful shame, and all the rest in order to have any sense of ourselves. This process begins at birth—no newborn 'decides who he is' apart from the presence of others to whom his little mind desperately looks to be seen and heard."[8] This is how we know ourselves, how we grow, and how we love. It's often how God "shows up" as well. It's where love shows up.

My testimony is still unfolding. The last three years of disillusionment with the church have shaken me up pretty good. I'm learning so much about friendship through this longer disruption to my story. I've learned something so profound and yet so simple: one of the most meaningful acts of love and friendship is simply showing up.

And that's really it. We can present our propositional statements of faith, but even they can be found wanting. I hold fast to my confession of faith, and it anchors me. These statements about who God is and what he is doing are like guardrails that help us more fully know God and to tell our stories.[9] But they are empty without our embodied presence. Mere words. What have we really learned about love in the church? Isn't the mission of the church to prepare our souls for love? What does that look like? Why does it seem that Christians are more attracted to power than love? Often, when our lives are disrupted, we can choose to pursue one or the other. We can let our fears lead us to grasp for power and control, or we can be vulnerable and look for love. In these times of affliction and disruption, we are faced with an underlying question of what really matters. So are we going to hold on to what matters, no matter the cost?

Love matters. It's the greatest commandment:

> "Teacher, which command in the law is the greatest?"
>
> He said to him, "Love the Lord your God with all your heart, with all your soul, and with all your mind. This is the greatest and most important command. The second is like it: Love your neighbor as yourself. All the Law and the Prophets depend on these two commands." (Matt. 22:36–40)

All Christians would affirm this. But in practice, what is our greatest commandment? There's so much ugliness in politics, in debates, in social media exchanges, and in our own minds and hearts. We quickly label those who disagree with us as a repugnant cultural other. "At least we're not like them." We are living in a polarized time, aren't we?

Let me ask you this: If your life were full of affliction, would you still love God? Would he still be good? Here's another question: If there were no such thing as a literal hell after death, would you still love God? Do we love him just so he will bless us with comfort and security? Do we love him because he will save us from hell? Or do we love him because he is beauty, goodness, and truth, and we want to be with him to be filled with his fullness?

Beauty matters. Truth matters. Goodness matters. Because Love matters. And this is who God is in his triune self and for us. This is the kingdom we are invited to walk into. We need a theology saturated in love that is embodied, shared, and storied. As partners in Christ's kingdom, helping one another see what's real means we are hunters and sharers of these treasures. One word used about how the faith has passed down through the centuries is *tradent*. We don't use that word much anymore. As the canon of Scripture was being written and formed, the stories within it were passed down through male and female tradents of the faith, meaning they orally passed down the faith from one person to the next through their testimonies and stories. And we behold the life-giving beauty that has divinely unfolded!

AN INVITATION TO BEAUTY

Theology is an invitation; preaching is an invitation; teaching is an invitation. They change us. The invitation can come to us wherever we are. Where are you? Many of you are carrying pain, loss, stress, betrayal, sickness, resentment, the weight of sin that you can't seem to face, shame. But you show up to church to worship God corporately. Maybe you don't show up anymore. Church is both a people and a place. If we go, we bring stories with us, all there in a shared room with shared people. The joy, the real, the terrible, the tragic.

We come with stories, often buried inside. One sermon won't fix us. But it can invite us, with our stories, into beauty. We come for resurrection. Beauty rises—that's the overarching story. Beauty is something we *all* love. Something we all long to behold. Something we all need. Something we all want to be. Beauty must be built into our DNA or something. We long for it.

But beauty isn't something we can merely write about in propositional statements. Beauty needs to be shown. It's an invitation, a beckoning. So, you guessed it, I am going back to the Song of Songs with an invitation for us to gaze at beauty. It is one of my very favorite verses in all of Scripture:

> Go out, young women of Zion,
> and gaze at King Solomon,
> wearing the crown his mother placed on him
> on the day of his wedding—
> the day of his heart's rejoicing. (Song of Songs 3:11)

Poetry, metaphor, and song help us see beauty in ways didactical teaching and propositional statements can't. Did you ever wonder why the Song of Songs is in Scripture? Maybe God wants to teach us something about beauty. Beauty is a theme throughout the Song. (We will get to that.) Beauty is really the theme of our lives. God is inviting us into beauty. Beauty beckons us.

This verse directs our eyes to Christ, the substance of our hope. Maybe you are scratching your head, as you can see it clearly says King Solomon, not Christ. Well, we need to know how to read the Song. Solomon is a key to unlocking the Song. The woman, whose voice is prominent, is seeking a king, like Solomon. But we get the sense that she is talking about someone even greater than Solomon, as she calls this the Song of all songs. Verse 1 can be translated several ways. "The Song of Songs, which is Solomon's" doesn't necessarily mean that Solomon was the author or the man in the Song. It could mean that it's written "in Solomon's style" or that it's "dedicated to Solomon," among other possibilities.[10] The Song references his world, even as he is sometimes a foil character in it (Song 8:11). He was the king who was a "man of rest" (1 Chron. 22:9), his name meaning "peace." Ultimately, it may be directing us to his greatest achievement, the construction of the temple, the place of "ultimate sanctity and deepest awe . . . perhaps the title suggests that the Song is one way of entering that holy place—even, the only way."[11] That's what the early church fathers taught, calling the Song of Songs the holy of holies of Scripture. The Song of Songs takes us to the holy of holies through allegory, poetry, metaphor, and typology.

God also does this in his design, creating us as men and women. He is telling us a beautiful story that we are a part of—a story of Christ's spousal love for his bride. This is what so many of those church leaders are missing in hurling out public shaming of God's people. Look at the man and the woman in the Song. What do we behold when we gaze upon the King Solomon of the Song on his wedding day and see the crown with which he is crowned?

The Song shows us a picture of beauty: Christ and his bride.

There are numerous modern interpretations of who the man and the woman are in the Song. But from the early church to about the nineteenth century, the Song was interpreted as an allegory of Christ's love for his church, along with the individual soul of the believer. The man in the Song, a king and a shepherd whom the woman continually calls "my love" and "the one whom my soul loves," is Jesus, the second Adam,

King of Kings, the Great Shepherd, the One who brings peace. In the end, we learn that she finds peace (shalom, Solomon) in his eyes (Song 8:10). We also learn that he is a great lover and husband—that all this was set in motion by his love for us. This is who we are beckoned to behold in 3:11. Together. And that makes us all the woman in the Song, speaking for the collective church and the soul of each of us individually.

This Song isn't like other songs. In a sense, it sweeps us up inside it. Our verse shows us a picture of what is theologically known as the Total Christ, *totus Christus* if we want to sound smarticle.* This is a notion that *Christ and his church are so united in nuptial union that there is no speaking of Christ without his church, and there is no church without Christ.* And we will not grasp the scandal of love until we begin to let this sink in as much as we are capable. Our bodies tell this story.

When Jesus rebukes the Pharisees, asking if they remember what they've read in the creation account, he asks, "Haven't you read . . . ?" Sure, they know the Scriptures, but they don't seem to get it—the meaningfulness of God's acts, of love itself—as they are trying to test him. Jesus paints the beautiful picture—the one we too often miss—of God's creating us as male and female. "For this reason a man will leave his father and mother and be joined to his wife, and the two will become one flesh[.] So they are no longer two, but one flesh. Therefore, what God has joined together, let no one separate" (Matt. 19:5–6, referencing Gen. 2:24). Paul picks up on this in his talk about marriage, saying that "we are members of [Christ's] body. For this reason a man will leave his father and mother

---

* An excellent word my oldest daughter coined to poke fun at the pretentious.

and be joined to his wife, and the two will become one flesh. This mystery is profound, but I am talking about Christ and the church" (Eph. 5:30–32). Profound is right.

Hold onto this idea of the whole Christ while we look at the typology of man and woman that points to this archetype. Typology is a picture that teaches us. It reveals the endgame. It makes visible the invisible.

OUR BODIES SPEAK BEAUTY

Let's return to the creation story for a moment, just as Jesus asks the Pharisees to. Here we see a testimony to the glory of God's dwelling place in the creation of the heavens. This testimony beckons us to where we want to be—with God in his glory-realm. Then God made man from the soil, breathing life into him. Woman is created differently than man. She is created second, not from soil. God made woman from man. Both the difference in mode and creation order tells us something. She is not from the earth. She is created second. Some want to teach us that means she is subordinate—less. Where is that in Scripture? Where is the beauty there? I'm going to invite you to look at the big picture that our sexuality tells. As a picture and testimony to where we are headed (people and place), the woman represents the second order—the final act of creation that we await—arrayed with the glory and radiance of the Son. She signifies the promise of his life beyond probation. That's what we see in the endgame of Revelation 21:10–12. The invisible is made visible.

Behold! Her very presence beckons mankind to our ultimate hope as the collective bride of Christ. Man was to pass through probation, with his bride, to ascend to the holy mountain Zion, which her body represents, "the bride, the wife of the Lamb . . . the holy city, Jerusalem, coming down out of heaven from God, arrayed with God's glory" (Rev. 21:9–11, see also 21:1–2). The first woman, his necessary ally and partner, was to be a corresponding strength in their mission to receive the great reward of eternal communion with God for them and their progeny. This is exactly what Satan attacked in his deception. But God is ahead of the story.

Jesus Christ, the second Adam, left his Father and his mother, Zion the glory-realm, to cleave to his bride and ascend with her to the holy of holies. Our bodies enflesh and signify this good news, this love. We are icons showcasing the story of the outgoing, overflowing love of the triune God. This is so profound that it's worth repeating: we are created to share covenantally in the Father's love for the Son, by the Holy Spirit.

The creation story foreshadows this. Woman is made from the side of man, who was put to sleep, a picture of the church flowing from the side of Jesus, who gave his life for her. We find this overarching story in Scripture, that heaven and earth will come together. God's people will have eternal communion with him and with one another in a new heaven and a new earth. Christ and his bride together. Typologically, man points to the means of ascent and union: the love of the Bridegroom, the incarnate Christ, who is the first to love, the first to give, and the first to sacrifice. Woman typologically points to the realm and people of ascent: Zion, the bride. And in the Song, we experience an explosion of this typology with the woman celebrating in it, teaching both women and men what it is like to be the bride of Christ.

Why use allegory to teach what is already stated elsewhere in Scripture? Allegories and typologies of Christ and his church do something to us—surprise us, delight us, stir our affections.[12] They integrate Scripture, showing us the radiance of these stories coming together, activating each other, and enhancing the meaning. We are left amazed by the Divine Author of Scripture and the beauty of his word to us. And we are drawn into it.

Now, look at this woman in the Song! She is full of delight, anticipation, and longing for the Shepherd King. When we read the Song, we can't help but to want what she wants. We can't help but to feel what she feels and to long to be a part of what she describes. The invitation to gaze at beauty in Song 3:11 gives us the full picture of the total Christ, *totus Christus*. I love the meditation from the Puritan John Owen on it: "It is the day of his coronation, and his spouse is the crown wherewith he is crowned. For as Christ is a diadem of beauty and a crown of glory unto Zion, (Isa. xxviii.5); so Zion is also a diadem and a crown unto him, (Isa. lxii.3)."[13] The crown pictures our value to Christ and the rejoicing that is mutually ours in the consummation of Zion.

We need to be directed to this picture because the *totus Christus* features both Christ's sojourning bride and perfected bride. As the sojourning bride, we long for fullness and consummation in union with Christ. Our hope is a longing. We are laboring in this longing, unlike the perfected, eschatological bride experiencing rest. "The Church remains on pilgrimage through this world, aiming for the eschatological goal for which she hopes: fully realized union with Christ."[14] The story our bodies tell of the spousal love of God also helps to direct us to this picture we are beholding of Christ and his crown. And our liturgy in worship helps direct and recalibrate us as we experience this time of the already of the inauguration of Christ's kingdom and the not yet of its consummation. As my friend Anna puts it so well, "We ascend and descend each week by faith as we are dismissed with the benediction because we are a wilderness-traversing congregation moving toward our homeland."[15]

The Song directs our gaze to the beauty of the total Christ, our spiritual reality, Christ and his bride in nuptial union.[16] Jesus uses language in reference to this reality, saying "Saul, Saul, why are you persecuting me?" in reference to Paul's persecution of the church (Acts 9:4). He doesn't say, "Why are you persecuting my beloved?" He says *he* is being persecuted by Paul. To persecute the church, the body, is to persecute Jesus, the head. Augustine developed this doctrine of the total Christ, using it as a sort of hermeneutical key as he preached on the Psalms.[17] For example, concluding his homely on Psalm 17, he says, "Now whatever is said in this psalm and cannot apply in strict terms to the LORD himself, the Head, should be referred to the Church; for here the whole Christ is speaking, and all his members are contained in him."[18] Christ and his church are so united that his words are her words; her words are his. The "whole Christ" is speaking in this way.

Herman Bavinck explains the doctrine of *totus Christus* beautifully, saying that the church is being filled with the fullness of Christ (Eph. 1:23; 3:9; 4:10; Col. 2:2, 10), and "as the church does not exist apart from Christ, so Christ does not exist without the church. . . . Together with him, it can be called the one Christ (1 Cor. 12:12)."[19] This kind of covenantal union is hard to believe! That Christ—that God—would unite himself this intimately with his people. Even as it is not fully realized and we need to be careful to distinguish that Christ is not united to the church in the same way as he is to the Father and Holy Spirit, we are in a real spiritual, transformative union with the incarnate Son by the Spirit. Is it merely metaphor or imaginary when Paul tells us that "we who are many are one body in Christ and individually members of one another" (Rom. 12:5)? What does Peter mean when he says that we will "share in the divine nature" (2 Pet. 1:4)? As Kimberly Baker says, "[T]o say that Christians are incorporated into the one body of Christ is much more than a symbol or metaphor; it describes the reality of a transformed relationship between Christians and God."[20]

The Son does not need the church to exist. He is Creator and we are creature. This divine distinction is important. But she is his whole mission in incarnation. The Bridegroom loves his bride from eternity. Is that not a proper description of the story of Scripture? And yet it is so hard for us to let it sink in! What is anticipated in the first two chapters of the Bible is revealed in the last two chapters. What a glory to behold, what a truth to walk in, which bursts open our understanding of Scripture, and what an honor that our very bodies as men and women participate in telling this story! As Augustine saw it, "The types and symbols of the Bible are to be immediately applied to Christ and the church, the cornerstone of Augustinian psalm exegesis. Then derivatively, but crucially, they are to apply to the lives of scripture's immediate readers and hearers. Exegesis is about closing the gap between what scripture says the church is and what the church currently is, on the way to its celestial destination."[21]

WE ALL WANT TO
BE BEAUTIFUL

Beauty is a theme throughout the Song. The first time the man speaks, he calls her "most beautiful of women" (Song 1:8). Two verses later, he is admiring her, saying her cheeks are beautiful (v. 10). Again, a few lines later he says, "How beautiful you are, my darling. How very beautiful! Your eyes are doves" (v. 15). And she responds, calling him handsome (v. 16). In another scene her lover approaches, calling out to her, "Come away, my beautiful one" (2:10). He repeats the same line (2:13) and then tells her that her face is lovely (2:14). When we get to 3:11, "the day of his heart's rejoicing," he directs our gaze to the bride with *wasf*, a genre of ancient Arabic love poetry that delightfully describes body parts using metaphors (e.g., "your eyes are doves"). And he introduces the *wasf* with, "How beautiful you are, my darling. How very beautiful!" (4:1). At the close of the *wasf*, he reiterates, "You are absolutely beautiful, my darling; there is no imperfection in you" (4:7). Later, the daughters of Jerusalem call the bride the "most beautiful of women" (5:9). They see it too now. The second time the bride is searching for her Groom and finds him, he exclaims, "You are as beautiful as Tirzah, my darling, lovely as Jerusalem, awe-inspiring as an army with banners. Turn your eyes away from me, for they captivate me" (6:4–5). That sets him off into another *wasf*. Again, at its closing, "How beautiful you are and how pleasant, my love, with such delights!" (7:6).

Beauty matters! Look at how much the Groom uses his voice to speak of her beauty! She says it first. So boldly. So confidently. "I am black and beautiful" (Song 1:5 NASB). Why? Remember *totus Christus*. Christ's beauty is hers. Behold Christ's beautiful bride! Why? She radiates his own beauty! I left out one of the verses where he proclaims the bride's beauty in order to tie it all together:

> Who is this who shines like the dawn,
> as beautiful as the moon,
> bright as the sun,
> awe-inspiring as an army with banners? (Song 6:10)

What a glorious verse! And there is a question for us, here. An important one. Who is this woman? This verse activates multiple others. Let's look at those to answer our question, starting with the endgame. Who else is described as shining? Jesus Christ. "He had seven stars in his right hand; a sharp double-edged sword came from his mouth, and his face was shining like the sun at full strength" (Rev. 1:16).

Later, the woman in Revelation is described with the same language, "A great sign appeared in heaven: a woman clothed with the sun, with the moon under her feet and a crown of twelve stars on her head" (Rev. 12:1). Isn't that familiar now? This reminds us of the language used in Isaiah, speaking of the restoration of God's people and the glory of the Lord revealed in Zion: "The sun will no longer be your light by day, and the brightness of the moon will not shine on you. The LORD will be your everlasting light, and your God will be your splendor. Your sun will no longer set, and your moon will not fade; for the LORD will be your everlasting light, and the days of your sorrow will be over" (Isa. 60:19–20). And "I will not keep silent because of Zion, and I will not keep still because of Jerusalem, until her righteousness shines like a bright light and her salvation, like a flaming torch" (Isa. 62:1). The bride in the Song is connected to this land imagery.[22] We see her typico-symbolic representation of Zion in this language. Israel, bride, and church—their hope is the same.

Beauty captivates us because it tells a story. It's the story our hearts already know and long for. Theologian Robert Jenson suggests, "Beauty is realized eschatology, the present glow of the sheer goodness that will be at the end."[23]

The bride shines like the dawn. Now, let's look at this verse again, noticing the military language ascribed to this woman:

> Who is this who shines like the dawn,
> as beautiful as the moon,
> bright as the sun,
> awe-inspiring as an army with banners? (Song 6:10)

This military language of an awe-inspiring army with banners, combined with the shining of the dawn, evokes another Scripture about Christ's coronation. In Psalm 110, we are let in on a mystery. We hear the Father say to the Son, "Your people will volunteer on your day of battle. In holy splendor, from the womb of the dawn, the dew of your youth belongs to you"

(Ps. 110:3). What a beautiful, awe-inspiring picture of the church, appearing in splendor like the morning dew. Behold the glory of God manifested in his bride:

> After this I looked, and there was a vast multitude from every nation, tribe, people, and language, which no one could number, standing before the throne and before the Lamb. (Rev. 7:9)

BEAUTY IS PREPARING OUR SOULS FOR LOVE

Beauty beckons us because it is preparing our souls for love. It also invites us to imagine where we're headed. Can you see her? The beautiful, multiethnic bride? The crown with which our King is crowned? Just a glimpse? Then you can see beauty in yourself, Christ in you. We are beckoned to participate in the great honor and calling of seeing and covenantally participating in beauty. It's an invitation into reality. Dallas Willard describes beauty as "goodness made manifest to the senses."[24] Of course the Song is full of speech about beauty, as it appeals to all of our senses! Beauty helps us see, reminding us of our trajectory—communion with the triune God and one another.

Beauty helps us see others through the eyes of Christ. We see that his bride is black and beautiful. Aren't we awe-inspired by this? That means we get in! We get into this path of beauty, which is leading us to the inner chambers, the holy of holies!

And we are called now to cultivate beauty in our spiritual lives, relationships, churches, neighborhoods, and vocations. In keeping with what we learned from Makoto Fujimura, repentance is provoked by an encounter with the beautiful.[25] Of course it is! Once we encounter beauty, we see how ugly sin is. We abhor it and want to shed it. We desire beauty. And what is beauty but Christ himself? As Augustine exhorts us:

> Let us therefore, who believe, run to meet the Bridegroom, who is beautiful wherever he is. Beautiful as God, as the Word who was with God, he is beautiful in the Virgin's womb, where he did not lose his godhead but assumed our humanity. Beautiful he is as a baby, as the Word unable to speak, because while he was still without speech, still a baby in arms and nourished at his mother's breast, the heavens spoke for him, a star guided the magi, and he was adored in the manger as food for the humble. He was beautiful in heaven, then and beautiful on earth: beautiful in the womb, and beautiful in his parents' arms. He was beautiful in his miracles but just as beautiful under the scourges, beautiful as he invited us to life, but beautiful too in not shrinking from death, beautiful in laying down his life and beautiful in taking it up again, beautiful on the cross, beautiful in the tomb, and beautiful in heaven.[26]

We get to behold this beauty! We radiate it ourselves as his bride! We are a part of it, as his body. So how can we cultivate this beauty now? We can recognize the invitation of beauty. Esther Meek says,

Beauty is epiphany. Reality is too. . . . When you get to the heart of reality, it is a *here I am*. It's fundamentally a self-gift of love. It's an event to which you are summoned to show up . . . not an item that you collect. It's not a characteristic of this or that painting or not. It's an event. And it's not an event of my own subjective personal taste. It summons all of me. It's not within me, it summons me to be beyond me, so it's ecstatic. So, epiphany is the Lord's gracious manifestation of himself to the Gentiles, right? You know, the magi, saying here I am. It's always self-disclosive. It's a self-disclosive event that then carries us beyond ourselves to desire and respond to it.[27]

This self-gift of love is the spousal love of God to his bride showcased, again, in the Song. God's gift of love is dynamic, fructifying, and reciprocal. We cultivate beauty by valuing it, wondering in its epiphany, and responding to it with our own self-gift of love.

Open your eyes in wonder over the beauty that surrounds us in our day. Beauty reminds us to pause and take in the present, evokes gratitude[28] for its gift, "reorients us to our deepest longings,"[29] and sends us out to create with it. Beauty is diverse and generative. Diversity is beautiful. Just ask the black and beautiful bride.

Makoto Fujimura helps us to understand that "we all must choose to give away beauty gratuitously."[30] That begins with directing our eyes to Christ, loving as Christ loves. He is preparing our souls. And we are only beginning to learn what love is.

IT STARTS WITH DEATH

My husband, Matt, and I have been friends with Jack for over ten years. Our kids grew up together. We know each other's stories well. They are intertwined. We've done a lot of laughing and crying together. We've learned a lot about love together. As we were hanging out last weekend, Jack shared that he is withdrawing his membership from his church and doesn't know if he will be going anywhere else at the moment. You can imagine, as I am writing a book about a church worth fighting for, how unsettling it is to have my own dear friends feeling overtaken by disillusionment in it. He shared that the church is so caught up in cultural and political movements that she has lost the plot in ways he cannot see her recovering from anytime soon. And the Bible has become a weapon in the cultural wars she spearheads.

Jack has a point. I knew it was a matter of time before disillusionment took over for him at his church. At this stage, we didn't have a good one to recommend in our town that would disprove his conclusions.

The church is suffering under disillusionment, disappointment, weariness, and corruption. Why continue to bother with it? Because God has already inaugurated us into his kingdom that is not of this world. We see the gaping wounds in the gap between what is already and not yet. Many of us bear the wounds. But we are not without hope. Rather, we are beginning to learn just how glorious and gritty hope is. And as we tell our stories to one another, our wounds begin to heal and scar. And our scars bear the testimony of holding onto what matters. The church matters to God. But maybe not in the ways we keep thinking of it. The inauguration was planted by the seed of his death. After all this talk about beauty, are you beginning to learn with me about how the church rises from it all? It is how we begin to learn what love is too.

Jesus provokes us, "Truly I tell you, unless a grain of wheat falls to the ground and dies, it remains by itself. But if it dies, it produces much fruit" (John 12:24). Is this verse not the picture of the creation of woman? And of the *totus Christus*? God keeps telling us the same story, in creation, in art, in nature, in our sexuality, in his Word. Let me explain. Adam was alone until he "died," in a sense, as he was put to sleep for the creation of woman from his side. He bled for her. His body was given for her. He awoke to behold her glory before him, as her presence beckoned him to. He awoke to sense the value of the means to behold this gift and come to know her. She was bone of his bone and flesh of his flesh. What a surprise! She was given through self-denying love. And the fruit is joy. It points to a much greater love of a much greater Bridegroom who dies a much greater death to birth a whole bridal church from his side. Now we are united with him in this. We are a body that is rebirthed and fruit producing through death.

Poet Malcom Guite tells the story for us in his poem "A Grain of Wheat," a meditation on John 12:24. It's a prayer and a longing:

> Oh let me fall as grain to the good earth
> And die away from all dry separation,
> Die to my sole self, and find new birth

Within that very death, a dark fruition
Deep in this crowded underground, to learn
The earthly otherness of every other,
To know that nothing is achieved alone
But only where these other fallen gather.

If I bear fruit and break through to bright air,
Then fall upon me with your freeing flail
To shuck this husk and leave me sheer and clear
As heaven-handled Hopkins, that my fall
May be more fruitful and my autumn still
A golden evening where your barns are full.[31]

What a prayer! How do we care for the Jacks out there, seeing no point in fighting anymore to hang onto the church? Are you a Jack? Is your church full of Jacks who are just going through the motions, losing track of what matters? What needs to die? Not only our expectations. Not only our politics. Not only our self-righteousness and self-*right*ness. We need to die to our *sole selves,* as Guite pleads. What Jack said sounds dark and dismal and scary. I know he isn't better off alone. But maybe in actually speaking out loud what he is sensing and seeing, telling us his story more truly, some of those husks are being shucked—not only from Jack but also from us as listeners. My sole self needs Jack to fight to love with me. My sole self needs to know what in the heck God is doing with all this. But I wasn't about to gaslight him and tell him that it isn't that bad. It is. Hope can look at the darkness. I also wasn't going to give him the sentiment of false hope and say it will get better if he just hangs in there. Instead, I died a kind of death right there with him. There we were in the *crowded underground* of disillusionment. Sometimes that's the death.

I'm trying to be careful not to butcher Guite's magnificent poem by applying it to something real and raw in my story. But art speaks that way, right? Things are not as they seem, and art gives us glimpses behind the veil. Here I see that when we get over ourselves for a moment, we get a picture of reality. How little we grasp of what God has on display! Living as we are in this inaugurated time, between this age and the age to come, we need to be partners and siblings helping one another see the kingdom that is not of this world. I'm beginning to learn that those glimpses often are given *within that very death, a dark fruition deep in this crowded underground, to learn the earthly otherness of every other, to know that nothing is achieved alone but only where these other fallen gather.*

That's when we get to see resurrections. Philosopher D. C. Schindler says that "in beauty, reality 'makes an appearance.'"[32] We can see the beauty of self-denying love in its gift. This is the reality we are invited into. This is true freedom. We too often think of freedom as a power: the power of our own will to choose, power over others, self-autonomy. But Schindler contrasts this with "freedom understood as *the gift of self* (in both the objective and subjective sense of the genitive here: in freedom, we receive ourselves as gift and we genuinely give ourselves to another),"[33] saying this latter form is what we need to recover. Rather than the sole-independent, noncommittal self we tend to foster, he joins classical philosophy in identifying freedom "as an intrinsic participation in the goodness that belongs to reality in its very being."[34] He urges that we come to know who we really are through transcending the sole self in this way. Do we value ourselves as gift? Then we will understand that "freedom, finally, has its truth only in love, in which to lose oneself is in fact to gain everything. And this understanding of freedom is itself the fruit of a recognition that reality *itself* is a gift that is good in its very being."[35]

In dying to our sole selves, we are given birth into Christ's body. And we can participate in the reciprocity of recognizing of others as gift and our self-giving needed for one-anothering. I don't have all the answers for Jack. That is part of my dying. I don't know how God is going to work. I do know that I want to sit in that underground with him, honor his story, invite him into what's real, and see what God has in store. I say this as if I am good at it. I'm not. Yet God continues to teach me and blow my mind with his beauty. That's what we need to point one another to. "If beauty represents an *invitation* to the real, and goodness our *involvement* in it in freedom, truth above all is our *reception* of reality, on its terms. It is for this reason a living relationship, one with the capacity to transform."[36] I believe this is how God uses our disillusionment with the church as a tool to direct us more truly to him. It helps us see the absolute powerlessness in our autonomous notions of freedom and belonging. He wants us to recognize ourselves and one another as gift. We are a gift of the Father to the Son by the Spirit. We see that in the crowded underground *where these other fallen gather,* where Christ died, and where he meets us. Then we are given eyes to see a much broader horizon of reality, breeding discovery and wonder, as our theology becomes saturated in love, and we will hold on to what matters, no matter the cost.

QUESTIONS FOR PERSONAL REFLECTION
AND GROUP DISCUSSION

1. What are the turning points in your story, disruptions or trials where you were faced with the question, *Who am I?* How did they "mess" with your sense of self and what you thought about God? What did these disruptions reveal?

2. In your experience, what have you learned about love in the church? When are you tempted to grasp for control and power rather than vulnerably looking for love? What is the personal cost to you when you do the latter? What has been your functional Greatest Commandment?

3. Let these three verses evoke your imagination: Song of Songs 3:11; 6:10; Revelation 7:9. Picture the *totus Christus* and the bride as the crown with which the incarnate Son is crowned. Picture who this woman is, shining like the dawn, as beautiful as the moon, as bright as the sun, as awe-inspiring as an army with banners. Picture the rising, beautiful, multiethnic bride as a multitude before the throne of God. What do you learn about love from these pictures? How does it help you "see" yourself through the eyes of Christ? How does it help you see others through his eyes? How does it reorient your longings? How does it affect how you see, listen, and look for beauty now?

4. How do John 12:24, Malcom Guite's poem, and D. C. Schindler's description of freedom influence your idea of the kingdom of God? Who is with you in the underground? How can you partner with them and give of yourself to them at this time?

NOTES

1. Bessel van der Kolk, *The Body Keeps the Score: Brain, Mind, and Body in the Healing of Trauma* (New York: Penguin, 2015).
2. "Integration . . . is seen to be the heart of well-being." Daniel J. Siegel, *Mindsight: The New Science of Personal Transformation* (New York: Bantam, 2011), 55.
3. So does Russell Moore. See Russell Moore, "The Body of Christ Keeps the Score," *Christianity Today*, August 4, 2022, https://www.christianitytoday.com/ct/2022/august-web-only/body-christ-keeps-score-spiritual-trauma-sbc-church-abuse.html.
4. Siegel defines the human mind as "a relational and embodied process that regulates the flow of energy and information." Seigel, *Mindsight*, 52. Notice that he refers to the mind as a relational process. He later states that our minds share energy and information flow through relationships, and that it is within relationships that our minds are created, "including the one we have with ourselves" (p. 55).
5. Annie Murphy Paul, *The Extended Mind: The Power of Thinking Outside the Brain* (New York: Houghton Mifflin Harcourt, 2021), 1–2.
6. Murphy Paul, *Extended Mind*, 16.
7. Daniel J. Seigel, *The Neurobiology of "We": How Relationships, the Mind, and the Brain Interact to Shape Who We Are*, Audiobook (Boulder: Sounds True, 2011).
8. Curt Thompson, *The Soul of Desire: Discovering the Neuroscience of Longing, Beauty, and Community* (Downers Grove, Illinois: IVP, 2021), 98–99.
9. This phrase about telling our stories more truly is used in Thompson, *The Soul of Desire*.
10. See Robert W. Jenson, *Song of Songs* (Louisville: Westminster John Knox, 2005), 2.
11. Ellen F. Davis, *Proverbs, Ecclesiastes, and the Song of Songs* (Louisville: Westminster John Knox, 2000), 239–40.
12. See Jason Byassee, *Praise Seeking Understanding: Reading the Psalms with Augustine* (Grand Rapids: Eerdmans, 2007), 51.
13. John Owen, *Communion with God* (1657; repr., Oxford: Benediction Classics, 2017), 55.
14. David Moser, "Totus Christus: A Proposal for Protestant Christology and Ecclesiology," Academia, 2020, https://www.academia.edu/38227535/Totus_Christus_A_Proposal_for_Protestant_Christology_and_Ecclesiology.
15. Anna Anderson, personal communication. Thanks to Anna for helping me develop this distinction between sojourning and perfected bride and how our liturgy ignites our imaginations.
16. For those wanting more advanced discussion about the ontological and qualitive distinction between Christ and his bride and dialogue with those

in the Protestant church who critique the doctrine of *totus Christus*, see Moser, "Totus Christus."

17. "Throughout understanding the Psalms as a prophecy of the mystery of Christ in his totality—of Christ, head and body (the *totus Christus*)— Augustine had found a hermeneutical key of expounding them, which enabled him to plumb the utmost depths of the Old Testament words and make them immediately available to Christian understanding." Michael Fiedrowicz, introduction to *Exposition of the Psalms*, by St. Augustine, vol. 1, trans. Maria Boulding, OSB, ed. John E. Rotelle, OSA (Hyde Park, NY: New City, 2000), 1:43.

18. Augustine, *Expositions of the Psalms*, 1:198.

19. Herman Bavinck, *Reformed Dogmatics*, vol. 3, *Sin and Salvation in Christ*, ed. John Bolt, trans. John Vriend (Grand Rapids: Baker Academic, 2006), 474.

20. Kimberly Baker, "Augustine's Doctrine of the *Totus Christus*: Reflecting on the Church as Sacrament of Unity," *Horizons* 37, no. 1 (2010): 9.

21. Byassee, *Praise Seeking Understanding*, 226.

22. See Rosalind S. Clarke, "Canonical Interpretations of the Song of Songs" (PhD diss., University of Aberdeen, 2013), 162–63, https://eu03.alma.exlibrisgroup.com/view/delivery/44ABE_INST/12152788870005941.

23. Jenson, *Song*, 46.

24. Quoted in John Ortberg, "Dallas Willard, A Man from Another Time Zone," *Christianity Today*, May 8, 2013, www.christianitytoday.com/ct/2013/may-web-only/man-from-another-time-zone.html.

25. See Fujimura, *Culture Care: Reconnecting with Beauty for Our Common Life* (Downers Grove, IL: InterVarsity Press, 2017), 49, 54.

26. Augustine, *Expositions of the Psalms: 33–50*, trans. Maria Boulding, WSA 3/16 (Hyde Park, NY: New City, 2000), 283.

27. Esther Meek on "Art and Knowing with Esther Meek," *Two Cities*, episode 61, March 24, 2021, https://podcasts.apple.com/us/podcast/episode-61-art-knowing-with-dr-esther-meek/id1502131405?i=1000514203917.

28. See Fujimura, *Culture Care*, 18–19.

29. Fujimura, *Culture Care*, 52.

30. Fujimura, *Culture Care*, 27.

31. "A Grain of Wheat," from *Sounding the Seasons* by Malcolm Guite by © Malcolm Guite, 2012. Published by Canterbury Press. Used by permission. rights@hymnsam.co.uk.

32. D. C. Schindler, *Love and the Postmodern Predicament: Rediscovering the Real in Beauty, Goodness, and Truth* (Eugene, OR: Cascade, 2018), 37.

33. Schindler, *Love and the Postmodern Predicament*, 51, emphasis original.

34. Schindler, *Love and the Postmodern Predicament*, 61.

35. Schindler, *Love and the Postmodern Predicament*, 63, emphasis original.

36. Schindler, *Love and the Postmodern Predicament*, 81, emphasis original.

FIGHTING TO LOVE CHRIST'S CHURCH

I couldn't get to the body.

We already stood out as first-time visitors in a tiny church. Frustrated and trying not to cause a scene, I whispered to Matt that my disposable communion packet was defective. The top layer would not peel, and Christ's body given for me was unattainable. We moved on to the blood. As the woman was coming around the corner with the trash can, Matt began to make it his mission to penetrate though the deceivingly strong film on my communion packet. Were we making a scene? Did everyone see how desperate we'd become? She held out the trash can and Matt, always the hero, was about to say something to her. Was he going to ask for another? Was he going to keep trying with this one? I motioned to him to just let it go. Throw it away. You could tell he felt wrong disposing of a sacred sacrament that way. When she moved on to the next row, I whispered, "It's okay. It's just a metaphor for my life."

My family needs the body of Christ, but it's elusive to us right now. There I was, acting it out in this scene during worship just as much as the story we enact together in the rest of the liturgy. "Lord, you see me. Why won't you give us your body?" Ironically, we sang "Nothing but the Blood" as the follow-up song. It was like Christ's words of assurance spoken back through the singing voices of the small congregation. His blood is enough sustenance for now.

It's been one year since we officially left our church and denomination, asking for our membership to be removed. Usually, when you change churches, you can keep your old membership until you find another church in which to formally transfer it. But our entire family agreed that we could no longer legitimize the denomination with our membership, even in name only. And I wasn't safe there. My elders and pastor would continually be hounded to file ecclesial charges against me or face charges against themselves. One pastor went so far as to post the link to our church on Facebook, with my pastor's face on it, asking people to call and email the church to urge them to press charges against me. Except there wasn't anything real to charge me with. It's all so silly. Regardless, these men persevered in their efforts to vilify me. Once they used a screenshot from an old social media post of me taking my daughter out to lunch after church before I was her first hair client at the salon that afternoon. They wanted to charge me for breaking the Sabbath. Imagine having church officers scouring your social media, and who knows what else, only to publicly shame you. Just to say, "See, I told you she is dangerous!" And imagine that these men are ordained in a culture that enables this to continue.

I wish I could say, "So we said, 'peace out,' and now we are in a thriving church community." This book is in the raw, during our search and fight to love Christ's church. It's been a disappointing year. Those of you who have been harmed by the church know how difficult it is to even go. Some of you are processing so much trauma that your bodies just cannot make that step right now. The very place and people God promised as a blessing to you has instead become a source of harm. I don't want to shame anyone who is suffering like this. God sees and loves you no matter what your church attendance record is. And if you are a church leader reading this, know that your community includes people with open wounds from church trauma. Instead of turning your nose up at those who aren't answering the call to corporate worship, consider exercising empathy and seeing how you can be Christ's body to them during this time. With consent. Not as a project. By being a friend.

The small house of worship, where the post-COVID-19 disposable communion cup would not let me receive the body of Christ that was given for me, was located on a street with old houses converted into upscale restaurants, coffee houses, and even a church. The small congregation had a little ethnic diversity, which pleased us. Mask wearers and nonmaskers existed together. The children's church room had a service dog. The pastor, an older man, sat while he preached.* The title of the sermon series was "Reconstructing Faith." The sermon was about grace and how hard it is for the church to accept it. After

---

* I later discovered this was due to a recent knee surgery.

singing the last song, that moment of awkwardness arose, one that our family knows all too well. Friends begin talking, and we wriggle there like bait, deciding whether to wait for someone to talk to us or to slip out the door. We've been slipping out the door more often. Standing there is such an uncomfortable feeling! Those of you who are reading and regularly in church, be the person who is pleasantly curious and hospitable. The pastor of this church was that person. He caught my husband right as we were leaving the room. So I turned around as well.

For the first time on a Sunday morning in quite a while, we drove home with some hope. It made me realize how afraid I am to have hope now. The church we've been looking for doesn't exist within a twenty-five-minute driving radius—our self-designated commuting limit to cultivate and serve in community. We want something confessional, in that it holds to the creeds that the early church confessed. We hope for some rich liturgy—a participatory order of worship that leads us by invitation, song, confession, absolution, sacrament, and prayer to spiritually ascend Mount Zion before blessing us in the Lord and sending us back out as salt and light. We are looking for a form of church government that isn't obsessed with power-over hierarchy and patriarchy, one that invests in every-member ministry while overseeing and protecting God's household. We are steering clear of churches that align with a political party and yet hoping to find a community that does speak into the injustice and the social challenges of our day. We want a church that is full of grace while also promoting holiness. We would love to be in a diverse community where we are truly sharpened and where programs don't replace personal invitations. We have no patience left for sentimentality or fundamentalism. Give us something real. No church face. No tribalism. No pyramid schemes targeting housewives. No conspiracy theories. And we can't in good conscience join a denomination that is revealing devastating patterns of enabling abusers. Sadly, that eliminates a lot of churches. We began to realize we are looking for a unicorn. Is it us? Are we insatiable? Has disillusionment rendered us unable to let people love us? This little church didn't check all the boxes. We know we won't find our unicorn. But we saw glimpses of that love, beauty, goodness, and truth discussed in the last chapter. What matters. But that hope that began to spring on the drive home was scary. It revealed the armor that I've been building as a protection around hope. She was weakened and barely holding on. She couldn't risk another blow. She was putting herself out there, looking for a church, but her hope was still in bed with the covers tight around her.

Maybe it's also true that the body can't get to me. In Guite's words from the last chapter, why does *my* sole self have to keep dying while so many others are galivanting around as if everything is happy and comfortable in the church? Don't they see what's going on? Why is my friend Jack so right about the state of the church? If we are the body of Christ, then affliction, abuse, trauma, and disillusionment in the church is not a private matter. As Wade Mullen says, "Abuse is a community concern." Those galivanting around in silence and neutrality are giving "safe passage to lies." It's "fraudulent beauty."[1] And I've been the galivanter. But those husks are being shucked. The good thing is, Christ does not leave us lying underground by ourselves. It's crowded down here. And he meets us wherever we are. Through the last year, Matt and I found others down here that we wouldn't have expected. In learning the earthly otherness of these others—friends, disillusioned ones taking off their church faces—we are learning that *nothing is achieved alone*. This is what the body of Christ looks like. God's been providing his people with each other even in the absence of beauty in the local church. As theologian Hans Urs von Balthasar put it, "Devotion to the Church in the present age will be, at its core, not love toward the Church, but love that is that of the church."[2] That is worth fighting for.

This helps me direct my hope. I hope not for a church to love. My hope is the Beloved of the church. And he is with his people. He shows up in the voices, hands, and hugs of others. So in our disillusionment with church and our struggle to find one, we can still give Christ's love to one another. And lo and behold, we find his body given for us. This is a good time to introduce Frederick Buechner:

> We believe in God—such as it is, we have faith—because certain things happened to us once and go on happening. We work and goof off, we love and dream, we have wonderful times and awful times, are cruelly hurt and hurt others cruelly, get mad and bored and scared stiff and ache with desire, do all such human things as these, and if our faith is not mainly just window dressing and fire insurance, it is because it grows out of precisely this kind of rich human compost. The God of biblical faith is the God who meets us at those moments in which for better or worse we are being most human, most ourselves, and if we lose touch with those moments, if we don't stop from time to time to notice what is happening to us and around us and inside us, we run the tragic risk of losing touch with God too.[3]

FITNESS TO FIGHT

We wouldn't need faith if we could see our hope clearly. We've learned that there is no Christ without his church. This is his kingdom. Christ and his bride. But unexpectedly, we find the rich compost of his kingdom in the underground. As we fight together to help rouse one another to this love, we learn that it is much more than dreamy sentiment. Remember, there's death involved in love. Buechner really gets this: "To sentimentalize something is to savor rather than to suffer the sadness of it, it is to sigh over the prettiness of it rather than to tremble at the beauty of it, which may make fearsome demands of us or pose fearsome threats."[4] This is why we galivant around without looking at the underground, much less dying to our sole selves to *fall as grain to the good earth*. Looking involves suffering. We enter others' suffering. This is where beauty rises. And it does because we need resurrection. In a sense, little resurrections happen all over. We can only see them if we take time to listen and look. Looking around, we learn that love gives grace, doesn't encourage sin, fights for what's real, and promotes holiness in one another. Above all, love looks to Christ and trusts he will work in us as a community of faith.

Often in the underground, when we are dying to sole self while facing disillusionment and the trials before us, we develop the fitness to fight for what's real and what matters. And, man, do we need grace for that. We have to die to our carefully curated self—the story that we want others to see about us and that we are even hustling to ourselves—and tell our stories truly. The true parts of ourselves make appearances when our guard is down, when we are laughing, dreaming, or showing empathy. As Lester Bangs in the movie *Almost Famous* put it, "The only true currency in this bankrupt world is what we share with someone else when we're not cool." But we want to be cool so bad that we don't deal in true currency enough. What does it take to convince us that this is a false belonging? What will it take for us to dig out the real longings of our souls? When we suffer, we don't have the strength to keep the hustle going anymore. Facing disillusionment, we see that our lives were far more of a hustle than we realized. And the goal didn't matter. Everything human and vulnerable becomes valuable again. Here our spines strengthen, hope is restored, and love is trained.

This is where my friend Javon found the strength to die to his sole self. The story he was telling himself[5] before he found the underground was that he was a faithful husband and father. Life was good. You put in the quarter, and you get the gumball. Then his wife announced that she'd been unhappy for a long time and left him, and he got a DWI. It had to be embarrassing for an upstanding, all-around great man who is involved in the church. He taught adult Sunday school (and high school, and served in the nursery, wherever he was asked). He was barely holding it together at this point. Javon's heart was torn apart over his wife leaving him. The pain overtook him for quite some time. Understandably so. He wasn't drowning in alcoholism or showcasing a pattern of irresponsible behavior. And yet the few beers he had one night out were more potent combined with his medication. He shouldn't have tried to drive himself home. The shame was all over him. Javon told his friends and the elders at church about it. All coolness was gone. The man was repentant and taking responsibility for his actions. Thankfully, it wasn't worse than that.

Javon was in the place where he needed strength to fight for what's real. Only, he didn't know what was real. Was his marriage ever real? Nor did he feel the strength to want the strength. He lay there clobbered in the underground. But we were down there too. What a privilege it is to be his friend, to be able to sit with him through the pain, grief, and despair and watch him rise out of it a new man—one with beautiful scars. But I'm getting ahead of myself. In the underground, Javon needed people who see him, people with whom he can be vulnerable, people who pray for him when he can't find the strength to pray for himself, people who remind him of what's real, people who imagine for him when he is too disintegrated to do so—all while pointing him to the Life Giver. We need these people in our lives. In facing disillusionment, we need people who listen, who offer safe connections. Science agrees. Trauma specialist Bessel van der Kolk teaches, "Social support is the most powerful protection against becoming overwhelmed by stress and trauma."[6]

Many times they can see and listen because they too are down where the fallen gather. Isn't this where we would expect to find those with whom we go to church? People who have died to their sole selves in allegiance to the One who gives new life? People who will not accept the sentimental "it's all going to be okay" and "this is all happening for a reason" platitudes because we know to count the cost? Rising is vulnerable, painful, dependent, and glorious.

A while later, Javon's pastor and an elder invited him to lunch. Ah, maybe they see his pain. Maybe they want to ask how he is doing, to check in on Javon, to let him know they are there for him. Maybe they want to share concern after the DWI. Is he drinking too much? Is he taking the charge seriously and understanding the weight of his actions? Since those of us who knew him could see that he was, perhaps they wished to encourage him that he will get through this with the people who care about him—and to assure him they are among those who care. All these thoughts were running through Javon's head as ways the pastor and elder may want to minister to him by extending the invitation. It made him feel good. It made him feel seen.

Lunch started with small talk. Javon is a witty guy but won't stay in the shallow end of small talk for very long. He probably asked about their families, and vice versa, and when they asked how he was doing, Javon would be raw. That's the kind of guy he is. Towards the end of lunch, the elder brought up the DWI, saying something about being satisfied with his response to it all, but that according to the Book of Church Order they *had* to give him an official admonishment.

That was it. Javon was invited to lunch as a checklist item. Can you imagine last month's elder's meeting? "Next item on the agenda, we need to give Javon an official admonishment" (months after it happened, as Presbyterians do). "Who will volunteer to do that? Ah, yes, it would probably be best for the pastor and an elder to do together. Okay, what's the next item?" The pastor and the elder were not taking time out of their schedule to invest in Javon. Javon was taking time out of his schedule so they can cross him off their list.

Javon didn't tell Matt and me about their lunch for a year. He quietly held on to it. He held on to the reduction of his personhood by those who were called to care for his soul. Turns out, he was an item of business. It takes a while to process something like that, something that seems so small but reveals so much. You don't need numerous church officers publicly shaming you to be clobbered and disillusioned. Javon was in a vulnerable position. He didn't try to spin any of what he was going through. He was honest and raw. And his pastors came along with the hustle. The curated church. One that shames after repentance. Officially. On the record. Over lunch.

But in the underground, we find love. From the foundation of love, we can face disillusionment in ways that strengthen our faith. One of the first gifts we can give ourselves and others is freedom to lament. Christ's bride doesn't have to be galivanting around all the time with a big, forced smile. He doesn't need a curated bride to witness to his love. His love is real. He wants us to be real. Lament helps give us fitness to fight for this. Many of the Psalms are laments. We have a whole book of Lamentations in the Bible. Lament helps us to deal honestly with the story we tell ourselves. Unlike selfish complaining, lament bids us to face what deaths we need to die. To our surprise and horror, they are often good things.

Like my reputation. We want to live a life that honors God and have that reputation. I want to be known for the love I give, not for being a Jezebel. That longing is good. But Christ knows me, and that needs to be enough. I'm still not there, but I'm learning. I'm learning that my longings are for something greater than a good reputation.

Like marriage. It was good that Javon wanted his marriage to work out. He loved his wife, and her abandonment ripped his heart out. He wanted goodness there. The ache of that is so hard to bear. And yet Christ is better. He is good. He will continue to fill us with his fullness.[7] Javon is learning that his longings are for something greater than marriage.

We lament the loss of good things. It's a death. Javon's ex-wife wasn't interested in his lamentations. As much as his friends are there for him, we fail. We can't hold it all. But out of the love he gave, the love he failed at, the friendships that give witness to his pain, and the gaze of a loving God who knows him and acts through him in ways unimaginable to all of us, Javon is gaining substance to his faith. The deaths are all part of the compost. We can't skip the step of lamentation. It helps us see what's real and mourn the deaths of the good things. Javon saw that he needed to lament his marriage, as the pain was so raw. He faced the pain so bravely. But the disillusionment he had in his church took longer. It was too much to bear all at once.

As we continue to think about facing disillusionment in ways that strengthen our faith, let's turn to the book of the Bible that addresses all our big life-questions. You guessed it, the Song of Songs.

CHRIST'S APPROACH

The Song features two night scenes. In them, we find the bride experiencing the absence of the One whom her soul loves. Sometimes it's of her own doing. Yet we see her fight through disillusionment and even abuse to find him. Let's look at the second night scene, which begins not with Christ's absence but with his approach. What she has in the beginning of this scene is security, which is a good thing and something we all want—in our faith, family, church, friendships, vocations, and finances. The Song is not a linear narrative. We find it as a dream, changing settings, scenes, and times abruptly and symbolically. This scene is placed directly after the hot and heavy consummation of their marriage that ends with the Father's blessing on the couple:

> Eat, friends!
> Drink, be intoxicated with caresses! (Song 5:1)

Things are as good as they can get! The following line changes scenes, and the bride is now snuggled in bed and tucked in her covers (like my hope on Sunday mornings). The Song takes us on another sensory experience. She says that she was sleeping, but her heart was awake. What a line! There's a tension there, right? We know how this feels. And then she hears it, a sound. She is excited to tell us that her love was knocking (Song 5:2). Sleepy security, desiring heart, and the sound of her lover's approach.

His words are so tender, heaping praise on her, waiting on her agency and consent.

> Open to me, my sister, my darling,
> my dove, my perfect one.
> For my head is drenched with dew,
> my hair with droplets of the night. (Song 5:2)

We could spend so much time camping out in this liminal space, at the door with Christ. How he calls her "sister," showing his honor for her; "darling," his special companion; "dove," the symbol of his Spirit descending on her; and "perfect one," complete and undefiled. This is how Christ sees his church. This is how he sees you. He invites intimacy and communion. More than that, he doesn't see us apart from himself. She is *his* perfect one. This is a bride in union with Christ. Picking up on the theme of *totus Christus* in preaching on Song 5:2–3, Puritan Richard Sibbes comments, "Then, because the church is Christ mystical, it is near to him; and, in a manner, as near as that sacred body of his, both making up one Christ mystical. And so is amiable and beloved even of God himself, who hath pure eyes; yet in this respect looks upon the church as undefiled."[8]

More senses are aroused. His head is drenched with dew, his hair with the droplets of the night. We see echoes of Psalm 110:3: "Your people will volunteer on your day of battle. In holy splendor, from the womb of the dawn, the dew of your youth belongs to you." So we anticipate her rising in that freedom in belonging. But instead of rising to meet her Groom, she chooses sleepy security over desire—well, at first, anyway. She waivers.

After all, she's all washed up for bed. He wouldn't want her to get her feet dirty. He wouldn't want her to have to put her clothes back on to rise and meet him after putting her security blanket on, would he? But then "he thrust his hand through the opening" and that got her feeling all the feelings. It's more powerful than that though. There are all kinds of echoes in this scene with the rest of the canon of Scripture, but one to point out here is where my translation says her feelings were "stirred" (Song 5:4). Ellen Davis notes that the Greek bumps fists with Jeremiah 31:20, where God is saying his guts heave and churn for Ephraim.[9] Her guts are heaving and churning for him.

Her hands are dripping and fingers flowing with myrrh as she rises and reaches for the bolt (Song 5:5). Ah, this myrrh reminds us of their wedding night, where he ends his *wasf* to her saying, "Until the day breaks and the shadows flee, I will make my way to the mountain of myrrh and the hill of frankincense" (Song 4:6). Davis explains what this myrrh tells us about the woman:

> Myrrh was the primary ingredient in the "holy anointing oil" that was liberally applied to the Temple building, its furnishing and vessels, and the priests. Frankincense was mixed with the grain offering presented by every Israelite, so the burnt offering would raise "a pleasing odor to the Lord" (Lev. 2:2). It's clear then, that the woman's personal "scent" is in fact the perfume of the Temple. The lover hastens like an eager pilgrim to the spice mountains, an image that beautifully evokes the curves of a female body and the Holy Mount in Jerusalem, where the strong odors of myrrh and frankincense call to remembrance the people of Israel's intimacy with their God.[10]

The Groom praises seven body parts of the bride in highly erotic language on their wedding night, pointing to the completion and perfection that he is praising her to be in our next scene (5:2). With this symbolism, she is associated with the mountain temple of Jerusalem. She is the aroma, the glory (Song 4:1–7). In our scene we have myrrh dripping from her hands as she is opening for her Groom. A pleasing odor to the Lord. One that calls to remembrance the people of Israel's intimacy with their God. But he is no longer making his way to her. In her hesitation, she's faced with his absence.

> I opened to my love,
> but my love had turned and gone away.
> My heart sank because he had left.
> I sought him, but did not find him.
> I called him, but he did not answer. (Song 5:6)

How many of us know this ache for the Lord's presence? The loneliness, the longing—it's a familiar theme in Scripture. The Song's tapestry is so embedded throughout the canon. I'm skipping much while showing you some of the threads. But this scene, with all its despair, takes us somewhere else. The disciple John was a singer of the Song. Maybe you picked up on the door knocking language. Maybe you can see how Revelation 3:20, "See! I stand at the door and knock. If anyone hears my voice and opens the door, I will come in to him and eat with him, and he with me," is bumping fists with the opening line of the scene in Song 5:2. Well, John also uses language from this moment of despair, this underground moment for the bride. Where else do we see a searching woman and a garden, frantic by the absence of the One whom her soul loves? In the resurrection scene told by John (John 20:11–18).

Guess what? We also see resurrection echoes of the "turning" found in Song 5:6. Only, it's strange in John. It doesn't make sense. We read that Mary Magdalene is crying, lamenting, at the empty tomb when she sees two angels. She turns around once and sees the resurrected Jesus without recognizing him (v. 14). When he calls her by her name, John says she turns around again in excitement, calling him *Rabboni* (v. 16). But in order to turn twice like that and still be facing Jesus, she would have had to do a whole twirl around. Why would she do that? It certainly shows enthusiasm. Maybe there is more going on. Ann Roberts Winsor calls these "bumps in the text"—something that doesn't make plain sense at first glance, causing the reader to pause and ask why.[11] Why is it there? Maybe it wants to recall another part of the canon of Scripture and enhance its meaning.

Winsor shows us that *turning* appears not only in our night scene but all over the Song.* We've already seen it: "Until the day breaks and the shadows flee, turn around, my love, and be like a gazelle or a young stag on the divided mountains" (2:17). At the close of our scene, the daughters of Jerusalem ask, "Where has your love gone, most beautiful of women? Which way has he turned? We will seek him with you" (6:1). From the Groom we hear, "Turn your eyes away from me, for they captivate me" (6:5). In Song 6:13, the daughters of Jerusalem sing, "Return, return, O Shulammite, return, return, that we may look upon you" (ESV). Winsor also points to "Come" in verse 7:11 as a word related to turning. And she says, "It is more than coincidental that the call of the daughters of Jerusalem to the searching woman, 'Turn, turn' should apply so uncannily to Mary Magdalene, the searching woman turning and turning."[12]

---

* An interesting difference is who is turning. Where we have a turning woman moving closer to Jesus in the resurrection scene, the man has turned and gone away in the Song. When read with the resurrection scene in John, the difference makes us all the more curious. His turning draws her nearer.

The connection of these two women turning and their frantic pursuits stirs our own guts to find who the woman in the Song is searching for. But she doesn't do it without running into trouble.

FACING DISILLUSIONMENT

I love how blunt the woman in the Song is. In facing disillusionment, we must name it. We must tell our story. And here we enter her night. The bride leaves a secure bedroom and goes out into the city searching for her love. She leaves the privilege of security that possibly led to pride or selfishness in hesitating to respond. What good is it if she loses sight of her love? And look where she exposes herself. This search is like a bad dream. We don't get the garden imagery that is throughout most of the Song. It all evokes a coldness. She calls for him and gets no answer. She can't find her love, but someone finds her.

> The guards who go about the city found me.
> They beat and wounded me;
> they took my cloak from me—
> the guardians of the walls. (Song 5:7)

It almost sounds like these watchmen were after her. The same line is in the first night scene: "The guards who go about the city found me" (Song 3:3). In the first scene, she seeks their help in finding her love, but they neglect her. Here, they violate and abuse her. They mess with her sense of self—or they try.

These watchmen are supposed to protect, not harm. Richard Sibbes refers to these as the "minsters . . . watchmen for souls," which calls to mind the true watchman and keeper of our souls described in Psalm 121:4: "Indeed, he who watches over Israel will neither slumber nor sleep" (NIV). What a contrast! The bride shares her painful realization. The shepherds, the supposed friends of the Bridegroom, are wolves. Foxes! What a nightmare! Sibbes tells us of the severity she is suffering: "It is a grievous thing to suffer of an enemy, but worse of a countryman, worse than that of a friend, and worst of all, of the church."[13] She speaks for so many in the church! This text isn't merely teaching us; it is doing something to us. Let's go to the underground with her and just sit for a moment. Look around. Whom do we see? We see all of those who have been disillusioned by the church. We see those abused by Christ's undershepherds. We see all those in Scripture without a voice, those "texts of terror," as Phyllis Trible calls them.[14] She is speaking for so many.

And it does something powerful for all of us. There's so much fight here. It rouses us all. Maybe you're wondering why I am going to the night scenes to speak of the disciples as partners in the kingdom. It's because we see all of history since the fall playing out in them. They function as a polemic. Here's the thing about fighting to love Christ's church. Woman, as she is a symbolic type to us for Zion/church/bride, has a story to tell us. We must look and listen. Sin has brought the worst kind of corruption, and we see it showcased so poignantly in the abuse of women. We see it over and over again in Scripture. And we see it today. Here's the story: if we do not love the Lord with our souls and our bodies, then we surely are not going to love his bride.[15] This polemic in the Song climaxes in the second night scene, but it's playing out in the whole Song. Do you see it? Rosalind Clarke spells it out, "Alone in the streets, exploited in her brother's vineyards, or mocked by the daughters of Jerusalem, she has been vulnerable throughout, even to those who ought to have protected her."[16] Behold the vulnerable bride. She is us! We see her persevere because the Bridegroom is preserving her. And she doesn't come out the same. She is transformed by going through the night scenes. We see her being refined in them. She is radiant. She *is* a wall (8:10). She sees real love, which is "as strong as death" (8:6). Clarke homes in particularly on how she speaks for women, elaborating:

> This woman speaks, in some sense, for all women who have been oppressed and abused. In the context of the Writings,[17] this includes the women who were evicted from their homes and families as the result of Ezra's edict, and the women who were written out of Israel's history in Chronicles. Denied any voice or identity elsewhere in the Writings, women who identify with these experiences find a representative in this woman. . . . Her suffering can stand for theirs and her voice for theirs, not only in her suffering, but in her desire.[18]

I think of the unnamed concubine in Judges, clinging to life at the threshold of the door, where the man, a Levite of all people, had handed her over to be raped all night long—in place of himself—by the tribes of Benjamin and left for dead (Judges 19:1–30). There she lies. We don't know at this point if she's dead or alive. We only get the voice of the man, who talks and acts to assuage his own agenda and ego. As Phyllis Trible memorializes the concubine from Bethlehem, "Her body was broken and given to many."[19] Am I being too dark, too extreme here? I ask you, what do we do with one of the most horrific and evil portions of Scripture? This night scene in the Song is a striking witness to the atrocious cases of neglect and abuse that we have in Scripture. It evokes that question of what we do with them and leaves it lingering in the air with the woman's words. But the bride is doing more than speaking for the women. The bride does something powerful. Her description exposes the darkness while revealing what is cultivated in that deep underground where she lay. She is, in a sense, still at the door with Christ. She's in a liminal space. And she shows us desire! She directs us to its true orientation—to the One who felt our pain, took on our shame, and poured out his blood, with *his* body broken and given as he clothes us in his righteousness and glory. It may sound crazy at first, the next thing she says.

> Young women of Jerusalem, I charge you,
> if you find my love,
> tell him that I am lovesick. (Song 5:8)

She speaks with such desperation and yet such authority at the same time. She speaks to whoever will listen, who may be in the underground, and charges them to join her search. The act of violence against her, at the hands of the supposed watchmen of her soul, further reveals to her whom her help will come from (Ps. 121:1). It intensifies her longing for her

Bridegroom. She charges them to tell him that she is lovesick. Are we this bold in asking for prayer? But the young women reply with the words that most witnesses would in such a state. Maybe they are mocking her a bit. "Why this man?" Why does she think he is different or better than the rest, "most beautiful of women?" (Song 5:9).

I imagine Mary Magdalene was lovesick too, looking into that empty tomb, frantically asking where the One her soul loved had gone. Can you imagine how your whole countenance would change after beholding the risen Christ? Can you imagine the joy in sharing this news to his other companions who love him so? Who thought him dead? And they didn't believe Mary (Mark 16:11). Did they mock her? Did they scold her? Did they think her mad? "What did he look like, Mary?"

The bride in the Song answers the young women of Jerusalem with a description that is fantastic—in the true sense of the word. It is like fantasy. She speaks of something otherworldly. Of resurrection. She's remembering and rising to newness at the same time. The *wasf* from their wedding night is brought back to mind as she describes her Beloved in a *wasf* with similar language (Song 4:1–7; 5:10–16). Why? She sees herself in him. *Totus Christus.* Her answer begins, "My beloved is white and ruddy, Chief among ten thousand" (5:10 NKJV). John Owen shows us the beauty in these words, "He is white in the glory of his Deity, and ruddy in the preciousness of his humanity. . . . He who was white, became ruddy for our sakes, pouring out his blood as an oblation for sin. This also renders him graceful: by his whiteness he fulfilled the law; by his redness he satisfied justice."[20] This language of whiteness is echoed in the description of Christ in Revelation 1:14,

"The hair of his head was white as wool—white as snow—and his eyes like a fiery flame." We see that both descriptions of the risen Lord are beckoning us to behold his glory. This is what the bride is to fight for—to beckon everyone to the One who has suffered for us and is able to save. He is worth it! This text evangelizes us, inviting us to participate in this kind of dangerous desire that brings us to our great reward.[21]

> His mouth is sweetness.
> He is absolutely desirable.
> This is my love, and this is my friend,
> young women of Jerusalem. (Song 5:16).

Now the young women are convinced and want to seek him with her. "Which way has he turned?" (6:1). She finds her love right where she knew he was all along: among his people. He's in the garden with the lilies.[22] It turns out that the garden and the graveyard are just one turn away from each other.

FIGHTING TO SEE

Here's the real fight that we are having: a fight to see what is real. This is why disillusionment can be a severe mercy.[23] It brings us to the door with Christ. It shows us that we've been using a security blanket. Even as I was writing the previous section, I heard from several friends and acquaintances in the underground.

One is a pastor who was found guilty on ecclesial charges

for false teaching, without the charges ever specifically being clear about what specific teaching of his was false. The errors that he was to repent of were never specified. This man is a treasure to his denomination. He sees the hurting. He defends the oppressed. Apparently, his writing about grace and forgiveness, love and care, was too much. But his accusers can't specify when or where. His family has been wrecked by the hatred and betrayal they faced in their own denomination. Shepherds are being driven out so that wolves can flourish. Today he informed me that he sent a letter for his name to be erased from the roll of ministers. They don't know what their future holds, but after sending that letter, he finally got a night's sleep. Still, he and his family are mired in sadness and uncertainty.

One friend is an academic. This dear woman has a brilliant mind and the life experience that pumps it with wisdom. She is humble, not one who wants to foreground herself. And yet she loves to be a part of reciprocal exchange and conversation. She could be such an asset to her church in theological contribution and teaching, all the more so with the passion and wonder that exude from her when she speaks about Christ. Sadly, the leaders in her church see her scholarship as a threat rather than a gift. It isn't much better in the learning environment at the seminary. She messaged me today lamenting that one of her last hopes for a male advocate, who has given her private encouragement but has left her to fend for her herself publicly, gave her the cold shoulder when she politely challenged something he said. She was left feeling the unspoken stigma of the threatening woman trying to usurp male authority—not the affirmation of a sharpening gift in communication.

Then an online acquaintance messaged me along with some others that a man in her church who advocates some of the worst popular offenders of abusive patriarchal teaching was recently nominated by her leaders as a candidate for eldership. She asked for prayer as she submitted her concerns and is awaiting a response. Of course, the nomination already reveals a lot.

Another friend reached out, weary from a social media interaction with someone she grew up with. Her hometown acquaintance was raging at my friend for speaking out about the abusive culture of their church and schools. When she tried reasoning with the woman, she was blocked. An ironic thing often happens in these situations. While this wrathful woman blocked her for naming the abuse, someone else from the angry woman's family saw the interaction and reached out to my friend for help. She is stuck in this culture with no frame of reference or tools to address what she is experiencing. My friend was up late listening to her story.

These are just the examples of underground happenings while I was writing the last section!

"I think we are on the edge of something new, and it will be glorious, so in that sense I am actually excited about the future." So says my pastor friend Wesley, the one who was found guilty of false teaching. He can say this even though he is sick over the evil being brought against his family while he waits to see where God is leading him next. Will his small church survive? Will his family need to move? Will he ever preach again? The waiting is hard. But the waiting room, the underground, the liminal space where Christ meets us, is also a developing room.

I am learning that waiting is an act of worship. It takes so much faith. And Wesley, in the midst of his pain, ministered to me with these words:

> One thing I've been thinking of and preaching about a lot is the idea of rest, of waiting for the Lord. I think we have the idea of righteousness as a list of dos and don'ts—that is involved, of course, but not really. Mostly, it is about waiting for the Lord's salvation and resting in him. Everything else flows from there. That is the whole point of the Sabbath—rest. A ceasing of the relentless activity and learning to sit quietly on your mother's lap (Psalm 131: "LORD, my heart is not proud; my eyes are not haughty. I do not get involved with things too great or too wondrous for me").
>
> This is why your work on the Song has resonated so much with me.

Here is a picture of the severe mercy I'm talking about. That picture comes more clearly into focus when we die to our sole selves and find that Christ fulfills us even in the underground spaces we've fallen. We need one another down there—Christ's arms and legs and torso and mouthpieces—to help us fight to see what is real.

It's challenging to write a book with a contemplative ask in a day that demands actionable content that can be marketed across diverse social media platforms. But I'm doing it anyway because that is where beauty is, and any action without it is empty. Practical maybe, but it can be empty. And it will end in despair. We need to die to our sole selves before our eyes are conditioned to look past the curated self. We need to see that our security blankets are false soul-cages. We need to see what's real before we desire the goodness of walking in it.

The contemplative work comes first, continually helping us to see what's real and to develop our desires so we can look at some of these practical matters in that light. I shared *lament* and *naming* as two necessary means to face disillusionment in ways that strengthen our faith. Both help us see what's real. Along with that, we need to see and to listen to the others in the underground. We help one another tell our stories more truly and dig out our inner longings. I'm going to close this chapter with some practical ways for us to move forward in and as a church. Above all, we need to fight to see what is real. We need to behold Christ at the door. Like the bride in the Song, we need to describe him out loud to ourselves and one another. Then his kingdom begins to come into focus, and we see that things are not as they seem. In that is the beauty, the invitation to enter into the real. This is our hope. It can be scary. And confusing. But we must rest in who Christ is, in his love for us, and in how he is preparing us for it all the more. This directs our desires and gives us the courage to actually be the church—*where these other fallen gather.*

TOOLS FROM THE UNDERGROUND

Maybe you grew up in the underground. Maybe you've been galivanting around the church thinking everything was hunky-dory, but now something disorienting has come into your life. Maybe you are a pastor or leader who has a conviction that the church is steamrolling more people into the underground than helping them see what's real. The good news is that the underground helps us see together. We find tools through our experiences that led us there and by sharing our stories with one another. But we shouldn't sentimentalize this work either. Disillusionment with the church can rock our sense of self and ability to trust again. We learn that we need to cultivate healthier forms of trust if we are going to belong to a community of faith again. We can't simply continue to believe in a system, the "right" people, politic, cultural mores, hierarchy, or any other false comforts.

Whether or not we want to face it, power structures are always at work. There is the ostensible government to which a church or denomination subscribes, and there is also often an unspoken power structure at work within it. Both need examining. Things become a little clearer in the underground. New discerning questions surface. Who represents Christ in the church—one person, a small group of people (often men), or every member? Who has a voice in the church? What spaces can they speak in? When someone thinks a little differently, are they shut down or engaged? Who gets to be in the room when decisions are made? Who is represented in these decisions? If someone is harmed by another person in the church, what are the processes to address it? What kind of care is in place through this process? Whose voice is magnified in this process? How long does it take? Are leaders the first to offer self-denying love and giving *power to* (equipping and encouraging the saints to minister to one another), or do you see them exercising *power over* (enacting a view of authority that is not of Christ's kingdom)?

There is no perfect form of church government. They are only as good as the people in them. We have the freedom to discern which one best aligns with Scripture and ministers to the needs of people today. But one discerning way to answer a lot of the previous questions is to examine church government from the underground. Remember, that's where Christ meets us. So why wouldn't those who are his undershepherds be hanging out there? How would that change their methods of government and leadership? How would that change what church looks like?

The underground perspective changes us. It changes how we understand the limits of authority. Authority shouldn't be something constantly exercised over congregants in top-heavy fashion. And it isn't for status. When the mother of Zebedee's sons asks Jesus if they may sit on his right and left in his kingdom, Jesus uses the moment to set his disciples straight. He says that his kingdom is contrary to the world's view of power and authority. Here is greatness: to serve, to put ourselves last, to give our lives for one another, dying little deaths to the sole self and watching Christ resurrect these grains into something beautiful (Matt. 20:20–27). Something interpersonal. Our selves are filled with Christ in our seeing the gift that we are to others and receiving the gift others are to us. We are authorized for sole self-sacrificing love. When our eyes are directed to Christ, we see his love for his people. Do we see our church officers leading the way in self-sacrificing love? How will this example empower and equip the rest of the church in reciprocal service? How might the church be encouraged in the freedom that Christ gives us to be a gift to others in sole self-denying love?

This freedom requires freeing ourselves from tribes and celebrity culture. Every generation has culture wars. It's so easy to get sucked into the battle, being led by fear, letting people tell us what to think or telling others what to think, whom to follow, whom to vote for, all the while missing sight of those in the underground. The others become repugnant. We hold tight to our sole selves, clamoring for victory, thinking we are doing something for Christ and his mission. How can we hold to our values without betraying them by our behavior? We can be led by love, not fear. Tribal thinking is faux belonging, not true community. It tells us what to think instead of teaching us how to think. It's rigid, disintegrating, and lacks curiosity and growth. You only belong if you wear the uniform and speak the lingo of their land.

Along with that, celebrity culture always leads to disillusionment. It doesn't stoop to the underground. The celebrity must be fed; its sole self is a mirage. Everything about it is curated. It's not real. It doesn't honor the earthly otherness of every other. Where is the beauty? The church is to be different. Recognizing this helps us avoid putting false expectations on others. We are down here in the underground, helping boost one another toward Christ. The bride in the Song was able to rise because her eyes were fixed on him. When the leaders turned on her, she lamented, named it, and refocused on whom she was seeking. When the daughters of Jerusalem questioned her, her hope seemed to only strengthen in who he was. She was lovesick.

That leads us to a scary step: taking appropriate social risks and leaving our security blankets. This takes time if we've been wounded. Open wounds need time and attention for healing. In that time, we find those who see, who we are safe with, who meet us where we are. Amazing things can happen there. Little resurrections. Something new builds. Our scars become part of the artwork. Scars form in our healing. They are protective, making boundaries stronger than the skin around them. Our scars tell a story. They help us get to the truth, past our curated selves, showing us something much more beautiful. We learn from our stories. Our scars are a testimony. I've learned to trust my instincts better, to speak up and say no when needed, and that people-pleasing is not the same as love. I've learned to identify and name red flags. And to be attuned to others who are hurting.

While I'm valuing my scars, the stories they tell, and how they help me to see what's real, I know that suffering itself isn't to be glorified. As one friend put it, "So much of violence is senseless and sinful, and I bristle with people telling me or others to find the good. That's so often a narrative of oppression. God will be there always and often most intensely in our suffering. Not because of it."[24] It's what Buechner said about sentimentalizing. We don't sigh and make it pretty, we suffer the sadness of it and tremble at the beauty of it, allowing it to make fearsome demands of us or pose fearsome threats. We rise to help others from being wounded, and certainly don't make light of it ourselves. What a great tension this is, almost nonsensical. I love how my friend Valerie clarifies it, "Hope in our scars centers hope."[25] Hope centers Christ, not the scars. We hate the wounds and wish them on no one. The scars, though, show healing, strength, resilience, and testimony.

So we seek people who stay in the room and with whom we can create beauty together. This is the good stuff: when our scars become part of the artwork. Isn't that what we see in Christ's own body? To show his disciples he was real and alive, the first thing Jesus does after saying, "Peace be with you," is reveal his scars (John 20:19–20). The story is there. They are a testimony. Christ rose from the dead. Christ loves his church. His scars made it into the kingdom. We can hold fast to that. He is calling us to join him in bringing us to his love and not to fall for a counterfeit. Still we fight for what Christ later told Thomas, "Because you have seen me, you have believed. Blessed are those who have not seen and yet believe" (John 20:29). We have not physically seen the living Christ and his scars. But we see him when we see one another, where all the fallen gather. He meets us there, and our bodies are made up in his as we love one another.

QUESTIONS FOR PERSONAL STUDY AND GROUP DISCUSSION

1. People in the underground are stripping their husks of the curated self. That can get messy. What might a church filled with these "other fallen" look like? What kind of nutrients would need to be planted in the compost for a church like this to grow?
2. What makes you feel secure? When you have this security blanket, are you tempted to any pride or selfishness? Is this security sometimes a crutch that causes you to hesitate in following the Spirit's leading in loving Christ and others?

3. Are there times when you ache for the Lord's presence, and you don't feel him near? How is your desire developed in this liminal space? How can waiting be an act of worship?

4. Have you ever thought about the testimony that our metaphorical scars tell? How do they help us see what is real? What do your scars testify in the naming of the injury, pain, healing, boundaries, strength, resilience, and hope? How do our scars help us to move forward, cultivating healthier forms of trust?

NOTES

1. Wade Mullen, *Something's Not Right: Decoding the Hidden Tactics of Abuse and Freeing Yourself From Its Power* (Carol Stream, Illinois: Tyndale Momentum, 2020), 178, 180.
2. Hans Urs von Balthasar, *Explorations in Theology*, vol. 2, *Spouse of the Word* (San Francisco: Ignatius, 1991), 36.
3. Frederick Buechner, *Telling Secrets: A Memoir* (San Francisco: HarperSan Francisco, 1991), 35–36.
4. Frederick Buechner, *Telling the Truth: The Gospel as Tragedy, Comedy and Fairy Tale* (San Francisco: Harper & Row, 1977), 36.
5. This is a phrase I adapted from Brené Brown, *Rising Strong: The Reckoning. The Rumble. The Revolution* (New York: Spiegel & Grau, 2015), 19.
6. Bessel van der Kolk, *The Body Keeps the Score: Brain, Mind, and Body in the Healing of Trauma* (New York: Penguin, 2015), 81.
7. Eph. 3:19.
8. Richard Sibbes, *The Love of Christ* (repr., Carlisle, PA: Banner of Truth, 2011,), 143.
9. See Ellen F. Davis, *Proverbs, Ecclesiastes, and the Song of Songs* (Louisville: Westminster John Knox, 2000), 277.
10. Davis, *Proverbs, Ecclesiastes, and the Song of Songs*, 265.
11. Ann Roberts Winsor, *A King Is Bound in the Tresses: Allusions to the Song of Songs in the Fourth Gospel*, Studies in Biblical Literature 6 (New York: Lang, 1999), 37.
12. Winsor, *A King Is Bound*, 39.
13. Sibbes, *Love of Christ*, 215, 221.
14. Phyllis Trible, *Texts of Terror: Literary-Feminist Readings of Biblical Narrative*, 40th Anniversary ed. (Minneapolis: Fortress, 2022).
15. See Aimee Byrd, *The Sexual Reformation: Restoring the Dignity and Personhood of Man and Woman* (Grand Rapids: Zondervan, 2022), 148–51.
16. See Rosalind S. Clarke, "Canonical Interpretations of the Song of Songs" (PhD diss., University of Aberdeen, 2013), 222, https://eu03.alma.exlibrisgroup.com/ view/delivery/44ABE_INST/12152788870005941.217.
17. The Hebrew Bible (Tanakh) classified books by the Torah (Law, Pentateuch), Nevi'im (Prophets), and Ketuvim (Writings). The Writings made up the poetry and wisdom literature: Psalms, Proverbs, and Job; the Five Scrolls, or Megillot: Song of Songs, Ruth, Lamentations, Ecclesiastes, and Esther (read in the synagogue in this order on holidays); and the books of Daniel, Ezra and Nehemiah, and Chronicles.
18. Clarke, "Canonical Interpretations," 218.
19. Trible, *Texts of Terror*, 64.
20. John Owen, *Communion with God* (1657; repr., Oxford: Benediction Classics, 2017), 49–50.

21. See Clarke, 219.
22. For more about how lilies are a symbol representing Christ's people, see chapter 6.
23. I picked up the phase "severe mercy" from the excellent book, Sheldon Vanauken, *A Severe Mercy: C. S. Lewis and a Pagan Love Invaded by Christ as Told by One of the Lovers* (New York: Harper & Row, 1977).
24. Valerie Hobbs, personal communication.
25. Valerie Hobbs, personal communication.

PART 3

PARTNERS IN ENDURANCE

5

THE LOVE
WE GIVE

I don't remember what I was doing when the doorbell rang. The interruption startled my sense of security inside the walls of our home.

In the fall of 2019, my whole sense of self was rocked. I saw what those church officers were saying and plotting online. Worst of all, I felt betrayed by an elder of our church, the one assigned to our family for shepherding. He was not saying things about me online, but he was participating in comment threads about me, providing random information such as details of our denomination—all while I was being slandered in the worst ways. No speaking up for me. No rebuking these fellow church leaders. No warning me about it. It felt like a deep betrayal and a violation of trust. Before, I was under the impression that his membership in the group was for my benefit, to keep an eye out in case the bad behavior toward me escalated, so I could be notified. It clearly escalated!

For a few months, my aim was restoration. I kept the pain to myself while having meetings with this elder, our pastor, and another elder. I silently hoped for repentance, some sort of explanation, and prayed God would help me to figure out how to forgive and continue to worship with this elder whom I used to call friend. Some of our closest friends were in the church. Even my parents. But we didn't share what was going on. For months, my family kept it to ourselves to protect the reputation of this elder and his relationships.

Earlier, I defined spiritual abuse as anything where you use your power to do or take from another what is not rightfully yours. While my elder was insisting that he was doing no harm, the things that were taken from me were not those easily filled out on a report. And it is dehumanizing to lose them. Loss of protection was a big category that I needed to break down: protection of my reputation, physical protection as jokes were made about a meetup in a remote area where I was speaking, vocational security as calls were made warning people who booked me to speak and misrepresenting my writing, protection in my denomination, and protection of my dignity and personhood. Do these things matter? Agency and power were also taken from me: power to be notified, power to defend myself, power to seek justice, and power for restoration. Then there was the loss of trust: in friendship and in the care of my personhood to an undershepherd of God. This all remained unseen, inside the walls of my home. Until the doorbell rang.

You know how sometimes we get annoyed when the doorbell rings. I'm not into fancy technology, so I don't have one of those smart doorbell cameras. An old-fashioned opening of the door led to a beautiful discovery—a gorgeous early winter bouquet of flowers. I thought, "Wow, my husband really has great timing." He knows I hate obligatory holiday flowers but love "I'm thinking of you" flowers. This was certainly one of those times where I needed to be seen. I needed beauty. This was a good-husband-points moment. Only, in opening the card, another sender was revealed. Our friends Pete and Maya sent the flowers and their prayers with them. On the previous Sunday after worship, I had said something to them about how the online harassment had reached new levels and that we were hoping to resolve a sensitive and related issue in the church. They must have noticed the turmoil percolating inside me. The flowers sent the message that I was seen and cared about.

It was a turning point for me. The following couple of years were revealing ones with a lot more losses. But those flowers brought hope into my house. Not the false hope that tells you everything is going to be okay. It was a "this sucks and you need flowers" kind of hope. It's the hope of joy because someone will gladly be *with* you through it.[1] The early winter of the delivery now feels symbolic. I was only beginning to learn that the security and belonging I thought I had in my church and friendships was more transactional than reciprocal, more fair-weather than built for hardship, and fashioned to support patriarchal power structures—the invisible fence that I was zapped on.

The deep wounds would stay open for a while. There would be all kinds of salt-rubbers reversing their healing. Addressing issues of basic human decency and common sense that, as my husband poignantly stated, "You don't have to be a Christian to get," was met with gaslighting and turning the tables to make me the bad guy. Every step of the process was shocking—the ineptitude; neglect; mocking; misinformation; disregard for the overwhelming number of receipts I provided in the form of social media posts, screenshots, emails, messages, and notes; kangaroo committees and bogus reports; himpathy;* accusations; minimizing; hearing from so many others abused in the church; lack of care for the wounded; and posturing after the conclusion, as if we should all be thankful for the work they did and the results they got. All the while, the only way I could use my voice was by keeping record of these public meetings and actions on my blog. A renowned expert on the topic wrote to say that I was encountering "gross spiritual abuse" and "that's putting it mildly," which was validating. *Yes, I'm not crazy. I'm not insatiable. This is really bad stuff.* However, I wasn't writing about the more painful side of it—the friends that outright betrayed me, and worse, the ones who played it neutral as if they were assessing two equal parties. Neutrality inadvertently supports abusers and allows the abuse to continue. I kept returning to this quote from Charles Spurgeon: "Leniency to the dishonest is cruelty to those whom they injure."[2] Their silence was cruel. It encouraged the harmful people and propped up the broken systems. Silent complicity is a form of neglect for the body of Christ. And it certainly isn't caring for anyone involved.

The pain from disillusionment is holistic. It affects our bodies, our emotional health, our ability to trust ourselves and others, and, therefore, our faith and our relationships. What a

---

* *Himpathy* is a term that is evolving but that centers on sympathy for male power over and against those harmed by it.

toll it takes! My friends' flowers communicated so much more than the words the little notecard could fit. I was seen. We had at least two partners to help us endure it. And that is a beautiful, life-giving gift. Flower deliverer must be a fabulous job, watching people go from annoyed by the doorbell to sheer gratefulness.

WHEN FRIENDS DON'T PLAY BY THE RULES

Fast forward almost two years from the flower delivery. Matt and I were at a local brewery with Pete and Maya. Mind you, we've just fast forwarded through many meaningful moments together. Many metaphorical flowers were delivered. And let's also factor in the COVID-19 pandemic that we were partnering through. It was the end of the summer of 2021, and we were no longer taking for granted the gratitude we have in the small things like meeting outside together with friends at a brewery.

That's when Pete dropped the bomb. "Guys, I need to talk to you about something. I've been struggling with my faith for a while now." He went on to talk about the details, but none of these words put together made sense coming out of Pete's mouth. We were stunned. This friend is someone we look up to, someone who's led us spiritually, someone we trust to share our struggles with and to help us keep *our* faith. And now all that he held true was beginning to shatter in his mind and affections. We felt we needed his strength during our disillusionment, and here he was coming to us, broken. It almost makes you want to run. How do you respond? How does faith endure? How do we show love and hold on to holiness?

Maybe you've had a similar moment. Or maybe someone you saw as a mature Christian fell into a serious sin pattern. Too often, it's too late. They leave with the wreckage trailing behind them. But what if they were brave enough to come to you? We might feel like we do not have what it takes to help. Frankly, most of us don't want to have these uncomfortable exchanges. Are we the type of person someone would trust their scariest struggles with?

I'm a reader and a researcher. I've got a bookshelf for apologetics—you know, full of all the supposed right answers and information to apply to what Pete was saying. But as he was speaking, I knew none of that would help. Pete's a reader too. He probably has some of the same books. It was deeper than that. This was about affection. And disillusionment. As Pete was beginning to face his disappointments with God, he was realizing that his precise theological grid of who God was supposed to be was off somehow. Living a godly life and learning the "right" theology wasn't earning him the relationship with God that he expected. Now all of it was up for debate. What is real?

If we want to face disillusionment in ways that strengthen our faith, both individually and as a church, we need to examine our preconceived notions about love. I'm an amateur learner here. But we constantly have opportunities to see, receive, and give love. They're not usually what we expect. Sometimes the love we give in these pivotal moments is listening without preparing the perfect answer while they're talking. Sometimes the love we give is to see people where they are and stay in the room. My husband is a teacher. One of the big struggles for him is the difficulty in measuring what he gave that day because results come very slowly over time. Relationships are like this. Some of the most valuable gifts we can give are holding on to one another's testimonies, telling our stories together, and letting God integrate our lives as our stories connect and ignite healing and growth over time. Love necessitates embodiment, a waiting *with*. Being in the room or, better, sharing a meal is a valuable gift. It's often about showing up and just being a partner in endurance. In this, we begin to tell our stories in truth, to gain courage to speak what's real, to stand up for others, and to dig out what we really want and speak it.[3]

Pete had the courage to tell us where he really was in his life and faith that day at the brewery. We were kind of scared. I was scared that our friend group was falling off the Christian wagon through all that had been revealed in the last couple of years. Other friends of ours were going through difficult times as well and would benefit from a functional church body. Should I have kept my mouth shut and let things continue? Should I have kept the curtains closed? Those were my first thoughts. Because I'm so self-centered. As if it's about me!

Second thought: What about Maya? This affects her as much as it affects Pete. After all these years, is she going to find herself married to an unbeliever? That's a completely different dynamic. What will this do to their marriage? If Pete's faith changes, will his values? Will his love? Does Maya have security in her marriage now? She must be scared.

Back to me: What about *our* friendship? Is Pete going to

distance himself from us now? Do you know how hard it is to find married couples where we like both people? Is he going to change? What about my husband? The Christian men that he looks up to for spiritual guidance have been disappointing him so much the last few years. Can he sustain it?

God, what are you doing!

The Christian life was supposed to be that we go to church, learn the right things about God, build good friendships with the people there, serve with your gifts, raise your kids in the faith, make it through a few curveballs, and give all the glory to the Lord. This was the ideal picture of discipleship to me. Sure, there would be crosses to bear. But Pete and Maya shouldn't* have this crisis at this stage in life. They've raised their kids. They've ministered to others. It's all backward. We all tried hard to find a good church. We served and wanted to grow there. How could this happen?

Look, I'm usually an idiot. I don't know how many people have come to me with something vulnerable, and my response was to try and download information for them instead of actually listening. As if my answers can save them from their pain.† While Pete was talking to us, and all these thoughts were firing in my head, what could only be the Spirit of God simultaneously provided revelation: "Aimee, I love you, but you're an idiot." (Okay, these may not be the words the Holy Spirit would use, but that's my interpretation.) Pete isn't a project; he's our friend. He wasn't something to fix; he is someone to love. His faith is wavering, but mine is not. And I can exercise faith on

---

* I used that word on purpose—wink, wink.

† Or more likely, save me from the pain of my own uncomfortableness in seeing my friend struggle.

his behalf. Part of that is knowing that God's got this. He is big enough to handle Pete's disillusionment. And maybe God is working in this very disillusionment to reveal himself in a way Pete never knew him. And maybe God will reveal himself to us in ways that we never knew him too. So I decided not to be an idiot.

I heard it put well in a sermon last week. The preacher said something like this: We do not grow by merely being given good information. We grow out of belonging.[4] Now that raises more questions: Was Pete still valuable to me as a friend even if he wasn't a believer? Would we still love him? I believe Pete needed to know this too. We needed to show him that we are staying in the room, that we will walk with him and Maya through this valley. So I didn't get into the debate about how Scripture was put together. Instead, I was curious as to what was behind these questions. What God did Pete believe in all these years, and how has he let him down? What does Pete really want? These questions needed unpacking with friends.

I didn't machine-gun questions at him at the brewery. We told him that we loved him. I took Maya aside, wanting to know how she was. We asked if there were any ways we could help. And because Pete and I do share in book nerdery, I later suggested a monthly dinner meetup between the four of us, going through a book that gets into these deeper questions. It's been such a rich time. We are all learning more about ourselves, and it has provided a safe space for Pete to talk about his struggle and for encouraging him to imagine God in a new light. But this isn't one of those "we did this book study and now Pete's faith is stronger than ever" stories. There's a lot of fragile pieces to tend to. We are coming to the end of the book now, with one chapter left, and it has been such a blessing for all of us. I don't want it to end. At the same time, who knows how God is working through it? I hope we are all getting to know the Lord and one another more and that our desires are being oriented to the triune God and his great love for us. Because discipleship is all about desire.

We've been learning about how the Spirit develops our desires from the Song of Songs. It's what makes learning about God—theology—so exciting. We are learning about the Creator, the triune, personal God who is coming for us. His kingdom is already breaking in. In this, we are learning the givenness of his love to us. And how it radiates from us back to him and to one another. His love invites and envelops us. And yet it is a love that is so patient with us. It doesn't take; it waits. Can I be patient with love as he is with me? Can I be patient with God while he's patient with Pete? Can I see Christ in Pete, even now, if I really listen and look? How gloriously curious it all is! I know we will continue to enjoy one another's friendship and the privilege of growing together.

TILL WE HAVE FACES

Many of us grow up in the church and still don't know what healthy discipleship is supposed to look like. Does discipleship mean serving in the important church programs? Knowing the right theology? Having the perfect family and the right friends? Living a moral life? Having it all together? Defeating our besetting sins? Becoming a leader? These are all tempting ways to try to succeed in the Christian life because we can deceive ourselves into thinking they are measurable. But discipleship is more vulnerable than this. Perhaps Pete is a healthier disciple than some pastors. He sees his poverty. As Richard Sibbes preached, "Sometimes there is more comfort in the society of poor Christians, than of the watchmen themselves."[5] We can spend so long in the church tending to our church face that we lose our actual face. We forget what we look like. And I've got to tell you that when Pete dropped that bomb on us, it shucked more husks from all of us. We came face-to-face with our own fears—especially Maya. We took a long look at our own status as disciples. What kind of Christian am I? Do I have what it takes? How is Christ shown in my life? What do I know about love?

That last question is developed well in C. S. Lewis's *Till We Have Faces*,[6] a novel that retells and reshapes the myth of Cupid and Psyche. The story is told from the perspective of Orual, Psyche's sister, who is writing a book of complaints against the gods. She builds her case, beginning with the death of her mother when she was a small child; moving on to her cruel father, the King of Glome; considering her physical ugliness, which she later masked with a veil; and reporting her undying love for her sister, her respect for her tutor-slave, her secret love for the married soldier Bardia, and her loyalty to Glome, which was proven when she became queen. She tells a story of how she sacrifices herself for justice and for love. It's a tale of loss. Orual would never forgive the gods for taking Psyche from her. Orual gave and gave, picturing herself more righteous than the gods. She knew love. She knew sacrifice. She knew beauty. She knew justice. Yet she was all alone.

At the end of her life, Orual has a vision. She is able to go before the gods with her case against them, with all that she had been documenting in her book. Finally.

Before the gods her veil was uncovered, and she was completely naked. Suddenly, as she was told to read her complaint before the court, the book she was holding seemed smaller. The pages appeared as angry scribble. But she begins to read. She reads of her hatred. She reveals that she would have rather her sister been devoured by the brute gods of Glome than what really happened—their beckoning her sister's love with a god that is beautiful. No one wants that. "We'd rather you drank their blood than stole their hearts. We'd rather they were ours and dead than yours and made immortal."[7] They dared to give her sister eyes to see their glory! Well, she refused to look. This was theft. Psyche belonged to her! What's worse is Psyche was happy there! Not Orual, she would have been happier to see her sister devoured by the beast than in this bliss, married to a god. On and on, she complained.

Until the judge cut her off, saying "Enough." That's when she realized she was reading the same thing over and over, from beginning to end and back to the beginning. Her voice had not been recognizable to her, and yet she became certain that this was, "at last" her "real voice."[8] There she stood in the silence. The judge asked her if she was answered, and she said yes. She explains to the reader:

> The complaint was the answer. To have heard myself making it was to be answered. Lightly men talk of saying what they mean. Often when he was teaching me to write in Greek the Fox would say, "Child, to say the very thing you really mean,

the whole of it, nothing more or nothing less or other than what you really mean; that's the whole art and joy of words." A glib saying. When the time comes to you at which you will be forced at last to utter the speech which has lain at the center of your soul for years, which you have, all that time, idiot-like, been saying over and over, you'll not talk about the joy of words. I saw well why the gods do not speak to us openly, nor let us answer. Till that word can be dug out of us, why should they hear the babble that we think we mean? How can they meet us face to face till we have faces?[9]

Now she sees too. She was all wrong about love. It wasn't something to consume or to manage. It wasn't measured out in fractions. It wasn't manipulated by sacrifice or emotion. It doesn't cage or control. She had her answer. "I know now, Lord, why you utter no answer. You are yourself the answer. Before your face questions die away."[10]

Don't we all struggle with our view of how God loves us and how we are to love others? Lewis's *Till We Have Faces* almost seems to be a commentary on 2 Corinthians 3:7–18. Paul is contrasting the ministry of the law of Moses to the ministry of the Spirit. The ministry of the law brought death in condemnation. But it was still glorious. So much so that Moses had to veil his face after he received it from God, as God's glory radiated from the law more than the Israelites could bear. It showed righteousness. With how much more glory, then, does the enduring ministry of the Spirit who *brings* righteousness overflow? Paul explains that a veil remains over the hardened hearts in the reading of the old covenant. The covering can only be removed by Christ. "Now the Lord is the Spirit, and where the Spirit of the Lord is, there is freedom. We all, with unveiled faces, are looking as in a mirror at the glory of the Lord and are being transformed into the same image from glory to glory; this is from the Lord who is Spirit" (2 Cor. 3:17–18).

The ugliness of Orual's face symbolizes her trying to obtain her own righteousness. That's what happens when our hearts are hardened, when we think the law of Moses, our own revised edition, is attainable. We are deceiving ourselves. And it sucks the life out of people. It's the love we take. We try to keep it wrapped up in our hands and in our hearts, but it turns black. We can't see that we are manipulating those who love us into serving our fears and perceived needs. We deceive ourselves into thinking that we don't need much. We cover it up with a veil. The ugliness of it all! We direct our eyes to other things like the virtues of which we speak.

But look at the freedom love offers. "Now the Lord is the Spirit, and where the Spirit of the Lord is, there is freedom." Many pastors are too afraid to preach this message. Its grace is too extravagant. What will people do if we let them know?

We are free from condemnation. We are *given* holiness, so we can walk in it. We are *given* the eyes to see its glory, so the veils can be removed. We are *given* beauty, as we reflect Christ. What happens when we see each other unveiled? It's like looking in a mirror at the glory of the Lord as we are being transformed into the same image. This is just too much, isn't it? This is what we want deep down. Our hope is being dug out of us as we look at our fears and false faces. We want the veil ripped off, and we want to see and reflect this glory. Christ in me; Christ in you. We want faces. We want to delight in one another's faces as we delight in the Lord together.

THE GIFT OF EXCLUSIVE BELONGING

We want to belong. But we struggle to find the freedom in genuine belonging and the love it gives. We see belonging as exclusive. We form our tribes and chisel codes of belonging on stone tablets. It's all very transactional. It reminds me of the brothers in the Song. During the opening of the Song, the bride tells us that her brothers forced her into labor, and she hasn't cared for her own vineyard (Song 1:6). They were angry with her. They made her work for them, to the detriment of her own vineyard. Throughout the Song, the vineyard is a metaphor of the woman's body and of sacred space (1:6; 2:15; 6:11; 7:12). The last section of the Song mirrors the first. We see the brothers back in the picture, and she responds by talking about her vineyard again. Solomon resurfaces as well, but this time as a foil character. While the brothers are trying to determine her character and how they will manage her, the bride has much more confidence. I would love to write about the military structures she likens herself to, but for brevity's sake we will need to skip over the fabulous line about her being a wall and her breasts being towers and focus instead on the vineyard imagery:

> Solomon had a vineyard in Baal Hamon;
>> he let out his vineyard to tenants.
> Each was to bring for its fruit
>> a thousand shekels of silver.
> But my own vineyard is mine to give;

the thousand shekels are for you, Solomon,

and two hundred are for those who tend its fruit.

(Song 8:11–12 NIV)

It's story time at the end of the Song! Solomon, the rich king and lover of many wives and concubines, had a vineyard in Baal Hamon. Only, that's not a real place that scholars can locate. *Hamon* means abundance, so we have this "lord of abundance" with his exclusive vineyard. It was so abundant that he needed to let it out to sharecroppers. Because of this, these tenants received earnings from the harvest. Solomon did not get all the fruit from his abundant vineyard. Two hundred shekels are for those who tend its fruit. Are we to carry on the metaphor here and think of King Solomon's seven hundred wives and three hundred concubines (1 Kings 11:3)?

In juxtaposition, we see another exclusive vineyard: the woman's. Her vineyard is hers to give. Go ahead and have your thousand shekels of silver, Solomon. That's chump change. As Havilah Dharamraj put it, "[Baal Hamon] is no better than the fool who thinks his money . . . can buy love. [She] can scornfully dismiss Solomon and his money and his women in three words: . . . 'Keep your thousand, Solomon!'"[11] Ellen Davis, who translates *Baal Hamon* to mean "'master/husband of a multitude'" or "'owner of a lot [of wealth],'" speaks to how the Song "throughout emphasizes the unique value of 'the one' (8:9; see also 2:3; 5:10). Therefore this name mocks Solomon as the poor rich man, whose silver and gold are only a foil to show up the superior wealth of love. Though master of many cities and lands, Solomon oppressed his own people and thus destroyed the empire (1 Kings 12:4)."[12] Not only that, but she also picks up on the metaphor of the vineyard and how it alludes to the husband of a multitude having to share with the "tenders of the fruit"—"the harem guards"![13] His exclusive vineyard wasn't so exclusive.

The bride is describing two different kingdoms, and love operates very differently in them. Or better put, love is revealed in the latter one. We see her declaring freedom from her condemning and controlling brothers, which is a freedom to truly give of herself in exclusive love. As Caryll Houselander describes, "Freedom *is* the possession of the inward Kingdom."[14] This exclusivity operates differently than that of the kingdoms of this world—it multiplies love. This is the good stuff: if we are in the exclusive union with Christ, then Christ is in us, and when we give his love, we are giving Christ to one another. Doesn't this blow your mind? Christ entrusts himself to *us*? We can see him in one-anothering? Houselander spells out the implications of oneness with Christ and why we can serve the holy sacraments as a church: "I saw that it is the will of Christ's love to be put in the hands of sinners, to trust Himself to men, that he may be *their* gift to one another, that *they* may comfort Him in each other, give Him to each other. In this sense the ordinary life itself becomes sacramental, and every action of anyone at all has an eternal meaning."[15]

Our love for God gives Christ to others. We are back to the greatest and most important command, "Love the LORD your God with all your heart, with all your soul, and with all your strength" (Deut. 6:5; Matt. 22:37), which Jesus expands to include "Love your neighbor as yourself" (Matt. 22:39). The woman in the Song directs us to something we are just beginning to learn about—love in the kingdom of God. Healthy discipleship is a reciprocal and dynamic integration of brothers and sisters in the church helping one another to develop our desire for the Lord together. It is all about preparing our souls for love. In this, we are "practicing heaven," as Dr. Curt Thompson calls it.[16] We are walking in the kingdom of God. It has eternal weight and meaning. As Dallas Willard put it, "The obviously well-kept secret of the 'ordinary' is that it is made to be a receptacle of the divine, a place where the life of God flows."[17]

How do we give Christ to one another? This oneness in Christ, his kingdom, must be on the forefront of our minds and hearts. We act out of that. We live in it. And then we see that we are sacred siblings and advocates, hearing, speaking, reading, and living God's Word in community. But we are not merely giving and receiving information; we enter into the *realness* of it, of the risen Christ. We don't offer Scripture as law or as a platitudinal sentiment to get us through our day. We are baptized into a kingdom, a kingdom in which Christ gives himself. We read and show up to our lives in order to see more of him together, and that transforms us.

We read Scripture as a community to receive and give Christ. Theology comes alive when we read the Bible with an eschatological imagination—that is, a wonder and curiosity of where God is taking us. That's what practicing heaven is, right? We are imagining where we are headed and living in that reality. In this, we are being courted and transformed by God's Word to us and for us. In this context, we endure together on the way. Church becomes a safe place to ask the hard questions about life, offering security as we express our doubts and provoking one another to love. Disillusionment happens when the church loses sight of what's real. John's words identifying himself as a disciple come to life as we recognize them before the risen Lord: "I, John, your brother and partner in the affliction, kingdom, and endurance *that are in Jesus*, was on the island called Patmos because of the word of God and the testimony of Jesus" (Rev. 1:9). This is why we are partners in affliction, kingdom, and endurance: because God desires to give himself to us.

Scholars debate whether Song 8:11–12 are the words of the bride or are the words of the Bridegroom. It could go either way. To that, I say yes! This is the *totus Christus*. Christ's words are the words of his bride as well, "my own vineyard is mine to give." This is our freedom in belonging to the exclusive love of Christ, the freedom and "realm of God's self-giving desire."[18]

FAITH AND SHOWING UP TO LIFE

This is the kind of love that shows up. It's what my friend Pete felt he was missing—God's affection for him. His realness. His givenness. And it kills me that Pete's experience in the church has been devoid of it, especially that it wasn't felt within our friendship. Do we blame God? The church? Pete's friends? Pete? My response is to want to help him look for it. To look for it with him—Christ in him, in his church, and given to him in our friendship and worship. I'm reminded of those words of Houselander, that God entrusts himself to us. It encourages me because I see how much of a failure I am at this, and yet I continue to get opportunities to look at ordinary moments in a sacramental way.

And we see Christ's people wrestling to see him and see what's real throughout Scripture. Were there ever any disciples as disillusioned as the two on the road to Emmaus (Luke 24:13–35)? Talk about not being able to see Christ—he was walking right beside them! I love this story. I glean new treasures from it all the time. Disillusioned on the day of Christ's resurrection, they have a lot to try and make sense of on the seven-mile walk from Jerusalem. When Jesus approaches and begins to walk with them, we read that "they were prevented from recognizing him" (v. 16). Did Jesus prevent them, or was their blindness caused by their own stress, expectations, and disbelief? They wouldn't have been looking for the living Jesus. Consumed by grief and confusion, did they give the man they encountered a real look? They were closed off by their anguish. And by their own arguments to try to make sense of it. We see the same struggle shown by the bride in the themes of God's absence and presence in the Song. The search is ours, and the revealing is his. It's always a gift.

The scene is a bit of a comedy, as Jesus asks these two what they are arguing about. Now they are talking to Jesus about Jesus, and they name their disillusionment: "They crucified him. But we were hoping he was the one who was about to redeem Israel" (v. 20–21). Oh, the irony in that word *about*, especially while they are walking with the risen Christ! And now on the third day since his death, "some women from our group astounded us" (v. 22). I always like to take a pause after that line to smile and bask in it a little. *Selah.* They continue with the testimony from the women who found the tomb empty and share the good news with the disciples that they had an encounter with angels and that Jesus is alive! Christ has risen from the dead!

At this point, Jesus tells the disciples how foolish and slow they are to believe. As it turns out, they couldn't recognize Jesus walking beside them and they couldn't recognize Jesus in their very Scriptures. This is our default. We need to know Christ to know the Scriptures. We need to see him present there. "Then beginning with Moses and all the Prophets, he interpreted for them the things concerning himself in all the Scriptures" (v. 27). Imagine walking those miles with Jesus. We learn later that, like the bride in the Song, their hearts were burning as he was talking (v. 32). Desire was being stirred. They prevail upon him to stay once they arrive at their destination. And yet it wasn't until Jesus took over as the host, taking the bread, blessing it, breaking it, and giving it to them that their eyes were opened. As Derek Taylor elucidates, within this setting of hearing the women's testimony, of their own disillusioned expectations and hopes, and of Jesus giving them understanding in how to read the Scriptures to see, know, and come to him, "Christ's gift of understanding occurs within the context of a historical narrative that gives it shape." But not only that: "The event of understanding is communal, emerging from concrete acts of togetherness, friendship, and hospitality. For the Emmaus disciples, understanding arises as Christ's own presence and their inherited hopes coalesce in a concrete act of bodily togetherness."[19] Immediately, they are compelled to find the other disciples and proclaim their encounter with the risen Christ (v. 33).

I can't give Pete the eyes to see. But I can show up. Now that Christ has ascended to the right hand of the Father, his Spirit, who he gives to his people, indwells us. The church is that sacred space in which we see the woman in the Song described. We are his body. We exercise our faith by simply showing up and giving his love for others with the expectation that Christ will show up too. This is what we do when we answer the call to corporate worship. We respond to his summons—with expectation. We are listeners and lookers. We find him in song, liturgy, prayer, preaching, baptism, and Eucharist. He interrupts our default systems to turn inward on ourselves. He disrupts us with his reality. He fills us with himself. This is gift. And we are sent out to give Christ. This is our nourishment.

That calls for concrete acts of togetherness, friendship, and hospitality. Showing up. What is your invitation today? We make faith harder and more philosophical and strategized than it needs to be. I say that as someone who enjoys philosophy and as someone who likes a good plan. But let's not miss the juice, the heart of the matter. Houselander has found it: "I have become *convinced* that all the splendor and mystery of our Faith, the sacraments and theology and everything else, has for its purpose just to teach us to be able to do the simplest and humblest acts of love in the least ostentatious way possible."[20] When we do that, we are both receiving and giving Christ. As Rowan Williams put it, it's "where God happens."[21]

LOVE'S SURPRISE

I'm becoming more and more convinced that the love we give is the ability to see what's real, what's breaking in. We are enduring together toward the full revelation of and living in God's kingdom. Seeing that picture gives us the desire to act. How much are we like the disciples on the road to Emmaus?

We read the Scriptures, we go to church with a community of Christ followers, and we miss him in his Word, right beside us, and in one another. He isn't alive to us. What expectation do you have when you go to church? What gets you out of bed? How is your heart prepared? Is it to encounter Christ with his people? Or do you settle for a practical message from the Bible that reminds you that he is cheering for you in your other life?

Recently, a friend shared with me the deep sadness she experiences in church. Nora feels like a threat whenever she contributes to the Sunday school discussion, which is really the only time she gets to talk in church. Her words are often edited by the pastor. And yet, there she was, bursting inside, stirred to share how Christ was so alive to her in the text they were studying. The pastor responded, "Now, let's not get carried away. . ." As she was lamenting how that made her feel, I thought, "Why not? I want to get carried away! I want the pastor to encourage this!" My friend is no novice to the text. She's more formally educated in theology than most of the elders in her church. Why wasn't everyone wanting to get carried away by what Christ is for us right here and now? She was doing the listening and looking for him and she was told, "Now, now, let's not get carried away"! The pastor refused to see Christ in her in that moment. He was essentially shutting the door to the kingdom of heaven that she opened (Matt 23:13).

On the other hand, Pete is struggling to see Christ. His words spoke out of a religious culture that presents God as the right information followed by the right behavior. The formula wasn't working anymore. The people in it didn't have flesh on their bones. And my default response was to act like my friend's pastor. I wanted to manage God for Pete. In reflecting on the teachings of the desert mothers and fathers of the early church, Williams puts his finger on it: "One of the great temptations of religious living is the urge to intrude between God and other people." Oh man, is that convicting. Intruding is something that needs to die. Down to the underground I go again. We need to leave behind the "deep-rooted longing to manage the access of other people to God."[22] These disrupting moments—both Nora's glimpse at the beauty of God for us and Pete's challenge to this truth—require a more honest evaluation of self and willingness to die to self so that we can listen and look for Christ together.

Remember the underground! The whole dying to sole self thing is kind of a repetitive deal. But good news: we're also receiving. We should be listening and looking for the risen Christ because revelation is always through him. And he is always gift. The love he gives reveals himself to us. But it isn't only my urge to manage God for others that needs to die. In the underground, seeing my friends there, I discover the patience I need to wait. Endurance is 99 percent waiting. You can't practice concrete togetherness without it. Patience is one of those things that I wish was for other people, but not for me. Patience with God, patience with other people, patience with myself—I hate it. That is, until I think about the incarnation, the cross, the resurrection, and the patient ascended Christ at the right hand of the Father.

Derek Taylor says, "Patience also underlies the very being of the church, for this unique community exists precisely because God has granted it time between resurrection and parousia."[23] This is a mystery—how Christ is transforming us into his likeness in preparation for his return and our eternal communion with him together. And we get to participate in it. Imagine God's great patience in that! "In this sense, patience is integral to the very logic of togetherness."[24] We are continually learning this mysterious logic as we are being formed together. The beauty of this fruit is glorious and is depicted in the words John described himself as: a partner in affliction, kingdom, and endurance. What a gift this is!

I don't think of patience as an invitation, but it is. Christ invites us to show up in our own lives and in the lives of others. In that, we listen and look for the door of the kingdom when it is opened, and we also try to open it for others. We long for belonging, and patience is key to the love we give in a culture of belonging that makes up Christ's church. He isn't renting out space to us; it's *our* vineyard. Patience acknowledges that we are distinct people whom Christ loves and whom we can learn more about Christ through. In patience, we are given the room to trust that God is working in and through us. Here, in this room, we learn that it is ludicrous to think we can or should manage him. Patience helps us get out of the way of the door to the kingdom of heaven. Knowing that we have a gift from the early church in the creeds of the faith, which keep us anchored in the core teaching about who God is, we can then acknowledge that God has so much to show us about himself through his Word as it intertwines with our lives. We don't only look to a few leaders in the church to learn from, as we come to understand the reality and the practice of the priesthood of all believers.[25] The church assembles in the underground. We share Christ with one another there. That's where resurrection happens.

And with patience comes curiosity. Here is a fruit, a reward even, of patience. We begin to see one another and learn. Think about the curiosity that Jesus showed toward the disciples as he approached them on their journey. He doesn't say, "Hey, knuckleheads. Look, I *am* Jesus, the risen Christ. Don't you recognize me?" He recognizes their emotional state. He asks them questions. He helps them tell their stories more truly. Jesus then takes their despair and reveals himself in the Scriptures before revealing himself in flesh and blood alongside them. He stirs their affections. They think they are inviting a stranger to join them at the table, and yet it is the living Christ who serves them.

Let's think about the table for a minute. What a curious and ordinary way to reveal himself! Christ used table fellowship as a primary means of teaching, particularly communicating his death, resurrection, and the new age to come. In his book *The Ongoing Feast*, Arthur Just Jr. reiterates that feasts in Scripture were liturgical events where God's people recognize his presence with them while rehearsing remembrance of the work he has done for their salvation.[26] These disciples did not anticipate the monumental feast in store for them. It's an eye-opening feast! In the Emmaus meal, we see a sign of continuation of this practice of table fellowship between redeemed sinners and their Savior.[27]

The invitation to Christ's table goes out to all sinners, misfits, and dejected. What does this imply concerning our attitude toward those we sup with? Just as in biblical times, table fellowship insinuates "peace, trust, . . . (and) sharing one's life."[28] How is this reflected in our churches and homes? When we pray, asking God's blessing and presence with us at the meal, are we reminded of that Great Day when our Lord returns? Does our dining together in ordinary meals and in the sacramental meal of the Lord's Supper cause us to look forward to the best feast of all? We often come together somber at the Lord's Supper, thinking about what it cost him, thinking about how unworthy we are. But the early Christians combined the Lord's Supper with a love feast, an eschatological meal amongst fellow redeemed sinners and confessors of Christ. Like the eye-opening meal at Emmaus, the future breaks into the present, and the age to come breaks into these last days. God's promises of the reality of the new creation are ratified in this meal. He gives and he gives.

But Jesus is patient. In preparing the disciples for this gift, Jesus does some preaching on their walk. When he was unfolding what we know of as the Old Testament Scriptures to the two disciples, they saw differently. But why? He was speaking to the same words they already had in their Scriptures. How did they not see it before? How was Jesus doing this; how was he revealing himself? This is the thrill that I am discovering about the love that he gives. It's poetry. And he uses allegory to help us see him. If you think about it, our whole spiritual existence is allegory, as we understand it. We *are* the body of Christ. We *are* the wild branch grafted into the olive tree (Romans 9–11). Our worship services and sacraments are full of allegory: baptism, the preached word of God, Eucharist.[29] And yet we are truly given Christ through them.

All the ways we communicate who God is are anagogical. The disciples didn't see Christ in the Scriptures. They were reading the words and events, but he wasn't there for them. Maybe we are in a similar context now. We are conditioned by critical scholarship, looking at the Word of God as a regular text under examination. We learn different methods to manage God's Word. We go to church, do our devotions, attend a retreat or conference here or there, listen to Christian podcasts, all the while missing the love he has to give. Jesus is showing us a way to look at his Word to us together with curiosity and wonder. Jason Byassee suggests, "It may be that we are now, at our current place in history, appropriately situated to see the way allegory ought to work. It ought to be aware of its own burden of bearing a certain weight of weakness with regard to the text, just as Christians' relationship to this book generally hangs from a thin thread."[30]

Have you ever thought of reading Scripture together as "holy play"? Byassee describes allegorical reading this way. It gives new light to the more didactic sections of the Scripture, surprising and moving us, "to demonstrate the beauty of the work of God in the world in a way that brings unexpected delight, and so to increase the love of God and neighbor." It changes the way we see. Through allegory, God makes himself present to us intimately in his Word and in life. He shows us reality and stirs our affections. He invites us to get carried away. We see the light coming from the door to the kingdom. "Allegory is then finally a way of prayer."[31] It is love's surprise. And it helps us see God's face, his goodness, and to patiently trust him with our daily offering from the underground.

And I learn that I have the body of Christ given to me. As we look for a church that upholds the core of the Christian faith and listens and looks for Christ together in corporate worship and with one another throughout the week, we haven't lost belongingness with him and his people. Each day is an invitation to listen and look for him together with those in the underground. I have so many friends there. Friends learning about patience, curiosity, imagination, wonder, and receiving and reciprocating the love he gives.

QUESTIONS FOR PERSONAL STUDY AND GROUP DISCUSSION

1. Reflect on how God entrusts himself to us and the power he gives us to give Christ to others. Have you ever thought of giving love and kindness to others as giving Christ? What is your invitation for this today? What deaths may you have to die to do that?

2. Have there been times in your life when you tried to manage other people's access to God? How about now? Are there any current circumstances where you are tempted in this way? Instead of managing other's access to God, how may you be invited to exercise trust and patience? How can you be more curious about what God is doing here?

3. What would listening and looking for Christ look like for you today? How would this help you recognize him all the more in church?

4. How might listening and looking for Christ together in the Scriptures and in the allegorical nature of our liturgy of worship surprise and delight us? How can this build our relationships and love for one another in the church? How does it strengthen our hope?

NOTES

1. "Joy means 'I am glad to be with you!'" Jim Wilder, *Renovated: God, Dallas Willard, and the Church That Transforms* (Colorado Springs: NavPress, 2020), 83.
2. Charles Spurgeon, "Pleading and Encouragement," sermon, August 17, 1884, The Spurgeon Center, https://www.spurgeon.org/resource-library /sermons/pleading-and-encouragement/#flipbook/.
3. See Curt Thompson, *The Soul of Desire: Discovering the Neuroscience of Longing, Beauty, and Community* (Downers Grove, IL: InterVarsity Press, 2021).
4. Josiah McCann, Catoctin Bible Church, October 16, 2022.
5. Richard Sibbes, *The Love of Christ* (repr., Carlisle, PA: Banner of Truth Trust, 2011), 224.
6. C. S. Lewis, *Till We Have Faces: A Myth Retold* (Orlando: Harcourt Brace, 1956, renewed 1984).
7. Lewis, *Till We Have Faces*, 291.
8. Lewis, *Till We Have Faces*, 292.
9. Lewis, *Till We Have Faces*, 294.
10. Lewis, *Till We Have Faces*, 308.
11. Havilah Dharamraj, *Altogether Lovely: A Thematic and Intertextual Reading of the Song of Songs* (Minneapolis: Fortress, 2018), 217.
12. Ellen F. Davis, *Proverbs, Ecclesiastes, and the Song of Songs* (Louisville: Westminster John Knox, 2000), 301.
13. Davis, *Song*, 301.
14. Wendy M. Wright, ed., *Caryll Houselander: Essential Writings* (Maryknoll, NY: Orbis, 2005), 88, emphasis original.
15. Wright, ed., *Caryll Houselander*, 37, emphasis original.
16. See Curt Thompson, *The Soul of Desire: Discovering the Neuroscience of Longing, Beauty, and Community* (Downers Grove, IL: IVP, 2021), 96, 211–223.
17. Dallas Willard, *The Divine Conspiracy: Rediscovering Our Hidden Life in God* (London: Collins, 1998), 21.
18. Derek W. Taylor, *Reading Scripture as the Church: Dietrich Bonhoeffer's Hermeneutic of Discipleship* (Downers Grove, IL: InterVarsity Press, 2020), 43.
19. Taylor, *Reading Scripture*, 17–18.
20. Wright, ed., *Caryll Houselander*, 192, emphasis original, from a letter to Frank Sheed and Maisie Ward, April 25, 1951, UNDA, CSWD, 12/12.
21. Rowan Williams, *Where God Happens: Discovering Christ in One Another* (Boston: New Seeds, 2005).
22. Williams, *Where God Happens*, 15–16.
23. Taylor, *Reading Scripture*, 165. *Parousia* is the Greek word for the second coming of Christ.

24. Taylor, *Reading Scripture*, 165.
25. See Taylor, *Reading Scripture*, 166.
26. See Arthur A. Just Jr., *The Ongoing Feast* (Collegeville, MN: Liturgical, 1993), 241.
27. See Just, *Everlasting Feast*, 241–42.
28. Just, *Everlasting Feast*, 133.
29. See Jason Byassee, *Praise Seeking Understanding: Reading the Psalms with Augustine* (Grand Rapids: Eerdmans, 2007), 50–51.
30. Byassee, *Praise Seeking Understanding*, 51.
31. Byassee, *Praise Seeking Understanding*, 51.

THE CLOSER I AM TO FINE

I thought I had a theology of love. One that was carefully learned in the narrow path of orthodoxy. Along the way, I've been caught up in the questions: *What does it look like to be a disciple of Christ? What do you believe? How do you live? Where do you go to church? How do your kids turn out?* What a funny story it all is, just trying to figure out adulting as a real Christian in the church: me, becoming an accidental author writing into this void I found of discipleship for women, being asked to cohost a podcast with a pastor and an academic, gaining opportunities to speak all over tarnation, getting all kinds of encouragement—as long as I stayed in my women's ministry lane. As long as I didn't pull back the curtain. And even then, as long as I didn't tell. Disillusionment hit hard. Everyone seemed to be playing a part, wearing a costume, keeping up the hustle. This can't be the answer to the questions I was asking. I knew that because I caught glimpses of the realness of Christ's presence with his people along the way. I actually believe the good news of the gospel, and I feel the beckon of its internal witness to follow him. With my brothers and sisters in the faith, I believe that he is with his church.

Then the watchmen clobbered me and left me vulnerable. The curtains were immediately shut and something had to be done about me.

A number of my friends began distancing themselves from me. The parachurch organization that I worked for demanded that I answer a list of questions by a group of unnamed men. These questions went beyond the confessions they held as their guiding principles. They were questions about the "nature" of men and women—namely, who's in charge. After seeking advice and responding that my writing speaks for itself, they said they "would be gracious upon my exit" from the podcast and blog hosted on their website. What a strange way to get rid of someone. With that departure, I grieved the loss of what I thought were real friendships. I grieved the disillusionment. Gateways began to close in spaces where I was formerly welcome. Some people privately told me that they support my writing, encouraging me to continue in this "important work," while they backed out of hosting me for speaking engagements and interviews because it may cost them their jobs or cause unwanted controversy. That is exactly how to keep things as they are. (More and more, I see the dilemma proposed in this statement: "It is difficult to get a man to understand something, when his salary depends upon his not understanding it!"[1]) It was terribly isolating. Is the problem that I am controversial or that the culture I am speaking to is hostile toward those they marginalize?

In isolation, there was still the whole formal process of addressing the slander and plotting against me by leaders in my denomination. And in my own church. That cost me and my family so much. Even now, even after leaving—or as I now say, escaping—I still have to deal with waves of men in these spaces trying to pull me back in so that I might conform to the very system that was spiritually abusive to me.

I have the scars.

So how can I say that it's funny? Dallas Willard describes laughter as "the automatic human response to incongruity."[2] Ha! Yes! Look how incongruent my quest for discipleship and belonging in the church is! How can we not find the humor in all this, even as parts of it are just plain cruel and, I would even say, evil? Treating a sister in Christ this way. Shaming her. Leaving her to fend for herself. Shutting the door. It's terrible! If I were unable to find the humor, to laugh with friends over the absurdity, I'd be lost in despair. But I still have to face it. That is the condition of Christ's church.

Willard reminds us that incongruity will be a constant in life—not always in such a cruel fashion, mind you. But because we are finite, created beings, we will always have incongruency before us. And therefore, laughter. He discusses the time Abraham laughed when God gave him the promise that his 100-year-old self would have a child with his barren ninety-year-old wife (Gen. 17:17). Hilarious! Sarah also LOLs at this news. Knee slapper! So God tells them to name their son Isaac, which means laughter. Then God says he will confirm his covenant with him, this laughter kid, as an everlasting covenant with his descendants (Gen. 17:19). What a joke! How incongruent with what we think life is, what we think our limits are, who we think God is, and what he will give us. And that's just it, the part that makes us laugh with joy. Willard says this is a "perpetual reminder that God breaks through."[3] Oh, how we need this reminder!

Although my laughter comes from harmful circumstances, I can look at my own story and see God breaking through all over the place. It helps me to see hope in my scars and to hold out hope for those who harmed me. Willard points out that laughter is a symbol of redemption, "for there is no greater incongruity in all creation than redemption."[4] The laughter in heaven will be fantastic. I love how this psalm depicts it: "When the LORD restored the fortunes of Zion, we were like those who dream. Our mouths were filled with laughter then, and our tongues with shouts of joy. Then they said among the nations, 'The LORD has done great things for them'" (Ps. 126:1–2). Later, using these words in her Magnificat (Luke 1:49), Mary inaugurates this praise of the nations. Laughter has come, and John is leaping for joy in utero![5] Caryll Houselander wondered, "It is amazing to think that in heaven when everything is understood we shall keep on saying to one another 'How astonishing that we should ever have doubted the mercy in it all.'"[6] I have partners in enduring to this kingdom truth. We laugh together a lot. It's agony and faith intermingled again.

Oh, the laughter, it percolates—I search for something only to realize how very small my questions were, how I was looking for the type of person that a Christian should be rather than for the personhood God is developing in each one of us in Christ. The whole picture looks different to me now. Hope is altogether different from striving, from perceived goodness, and from our wretched nostalgia and optimism. Hope looks at the same picture and sees something else: what's real—the husks and the deadness of them. Hope tells us where we do not belong. Like faith, hope resides near our anguish, the anguish of knowing how glorious we and the whole world are to be and how we are turned the wrong way. We must feel it, grieve it, and look again. This is all part of the glory of repentance.

What do we then see? Too often we've been seeing distortions of reality. Or we see only what we want to see. We've been looking through the rose-tinted glasses of our pretty, well-designed "managed reality" of goodness.[7] We are looking to the husks. The disruption of hope usually comes in the wake of a major incongruency with our lenses—a harm, a tragic event, an unmanaged memory breaking through the story we tell ourselves. And it invites us to look again. When we look, we see church better too. We see that this invitation of hope comes to us in the basic, concrete elements that make up the church's symbols, helping us see the husks that need shucking. They beckon us to question, *Why do we come? Whom do we want to belong to and with? What will we do for true communion? How did we lose it?* These symbols call forth our senses of sight, smell, touch, hearing, and taste.

Are we coming for nostalgia? For assurance? For the husks of what we think is important and godly?[8] For the husks of whom we think we should be? Corporate worship invites us to return to the scene each week and look again. At our baptism with simple water—where the promise is sealed with God's words to us, "You belong"—living water flows. Remember how thirsty you are. Look again at the bread and wine given to us together. "Until he come."[9] Remember the table. Remember his promise and his fellowship with us. In calling us to a prophetic

imagination, Walter Brueggemann tells us that "hope is sub-
versive." The picture of the present isn't what we want it to
be; it's both darker and more glorious. It cannot be "co-opted
by the managers of this age." Hope "limits the grandiose pre-
tension of the present, daring to announce that the present to
which we have all made commitments is now called into question."[10] Look again to where the other fallen gather. The simple
elements of worship can reveal how we see our lives, our landscape, and our memories. Let them be a mirror to reveal what
needs shucked away so that we might see differently.

I had the picture all wrong. Like Orual before the gods and
the prayer of Guite's poem, I attached meaning to the husks.
Turns out, I was showing up for things that needed shedding.
Death needed to happen: of my ideals and of my absurd belief
that Christian discipleship is just one picture for us all to
follow. My old sense of belonging was a matter of knowing
precise doctrines. And I believed that justifying myself was
going to set it all straight when the watchmen came after me.
I had been holding onto meaningless husks that hide clarity.
Rowan Williams quotes desert church father John the Dwarf,
helping us get right-side out again:

> We have put aside the easy burden,
> which is self-accusation, and weighted ourselves down
> with the heavy one, self-justification.[11]

What's beautiful about this is also terrifying. Resting in
faith, in Christ himself, takes over our fear-based grasping for
control, what people think of us, and even what God thinks
of us. Too often we would clamor to find our place in the

story and try to maintain the hustle of "good enough." It's all a cloudy façade, blocking our vision of the way of the cross. Williams recognizes how we imagine the way of the cross to be too heavy to bear. The humor of it all! The cross is light for us since Jesus bore its full load. We look at it as something we hope to begin to bear as we grow spiritually, like something we ascend to. It's too heavy right now; we have to grow into it. We're looking up for strength and missing it underneath us. The cross is at the underground where we die to our sole selves. As Williams put it, "Letting our best-loved pictures of ourselves and our achievements die, trying to live without the protections we are used to feels like hell most of the time. But the real hell is never to be able to rest from the labors of self-defense."[12]

What a blessing and a gift it is to see this beauty, to laugh at the incongruency of our limits and God's faithful love. I grieve that I have a number of what many would call enemies. But I've come to a place where I hope they will be able to see the incongruency as well. It took a lot of work on God's part to get me there. My pride is a thick barrier. Don't get me wrong, I won't be in the rooms where the curtains are closed to our own deeds done in darkness, trying to run the kingdom of God in human fashion. What an absurdity! I hope those stuck in those dark rooms will recognize it and join us in the underground, where God's beauty opens up to us.

Laughter reminds me that we are spiritual beings. The kingdom of God requires new life in the Spirit to enter. It's something we can't do for ourselves or for others. In Christ we are rebirthed into his kingdom in union with him. That's why spiritual abuse is so hard to recover from. My painful experiences reveal how little our spiritual selves or our personhood are taken into account.

I grieve this. We are not participating in the reality that is our spiritual siblingship in Christ. We can't do discipleship alone. But we find our companions in the underground, with husks beginning to peel. That's where the resurrections are happening and where God happens.

> Within that very death, a dark fruition
> Deep in this crowded underground, to learn
> The earthly otherness of every other,
> To know that nothing is achieved alone
> But only where these other fallen gather.[13]

What a gift to find the gathered other fallen in their *earthly otherness*—their unique personhood with stories of how they found it and how God is breaking through. We learn what it means to have spiritual siblings, and in that we are learning about Christ and being transformed into his likeness together. This colearning makes us more ourselves. It frees us to live according to reality and who we really are. We give our sole selves to one another. We hold the door of the kingdom open wide and speak to one another about the wonders we discover there: Christ in me, Christ in you, Christ in us. As Bonhoeffer put it, "We have one another only through Christ, but through Christ we do have one another, wholly, and for all eternity."[14]

As God's kingdom is breaking in, we are training for eternity, preparing one another in Christ for communion with the triune God and with one another. Do we believe this is real? Do we make up a mystical body, the *totus Christus*? As we saw from Bavinck earlier, the fullness "that dwells in Christ must also dwell in the church," and she "is being filled with all the fullness of God (Eph. 3:19; Col. 2:2, 10)."[15] It sounds too incongruent with our finitude to be real! What if we can help one another imagine what the redeemed community will be on that day, when our dross is fully purged and we are enabled to fully love one another? What if we don't just look at heaven as the place we want to go when we die, alongside the other good people or people smart enough to lock God in on a prayer, but we see heaven as a habitation of God and the glory-cloud of the Spirit, characterized by perfect love, brothers and sisters dwelling in the environment of perfect belonging to Christ with one another?[16] Then we will learn the truth of how we need one another to see Christ and ourselves.

There is so much to learn! Let us laugh together in it all.

WHAT WE REALLY WANT

A great tension and mystery exists between God's nearness to us by his Spirit and his farness from us in holiness and in the heavens. We clamor to crack the code that is the life of faith and obedience. We are finite beings with eternity on our hearts. The writer of Ecclesiastes sums up our condition perfectly: "He has made everything appropriate in its time. He has also put eternity in their hearts, but no one can discover the work God has done from beginning to end" (Eccl. 3:11). We look to the church to help us on the way.

We try to be what we think Christ wants from us.

Disillusioned, we find that we are not merely psychic selves in human flesh, who work, possibly marry, and contribute to society.[17] We find that virtue is not equivalent to uncontroversial homogeny.[18] Our value isn't measured in what roles we play or what we produce. Now we don't want to settle anymore because we ache for something otherworldly. We are spiritual selves. We need to share our stories to make sense of everything. And what we find is that our experiences, how we narrate them, and how often we stumble about and fail, are only the backstory to glorification.

What we really want is something so unbelievable that we do not dare to allow ourselves to dig it out. It doesn't sound appropriate. We try to stuff it down, this overwhelming, ecstatic longing. But we don't understand it or its power. We try to manage it and reduce it, settling for counterfeits. We long for its sublime and transformational goodness so we end up perverting it. It's more than love. I'm talking about *eros*. That's what we all want. We want into the inner chambers of the King, and we want the kisses of his mouth. We want him to open the door for us. The woman in the Song immodestly begins with this bold request:

> Oh, that he would kiss me with the kisses of his mouth!
> For your caresses are more delightful than wine.
> The fragrance of your perfume is intoxicating;
> your name is perfume poured out.
> No wonder young women adore you.
> Take me with you—let's hurry.
> Oh that the king would bring me to his chambers.
>
> (Song 1:2–4)

She digs it out for us. When the husks are shucked, we realize this is the real purpose and fulfillment of it all. My chapter title is a hat tip to an Indigo Girls song. They were searching for meaning in life too. Everywhere they went—the mountain, the children, the doctor, the fountain, philosophers, the Bible, and the bar—they came up empty. They found ease in saying there are no definitive answers, and the more they grasp this fact, the closer they are to fine. I can hear Paul's echo, "If the dead are not raised, 'Let us eat and drink, for tomorrow we die'" (1 Cor. 15:32).[19] Party on, friends. Life is meaningless. They went to the Bible but didn't see the door opened to them. They couldn't fulfill that inner longing. We need eschatological imagination to understand what we want because it will not be fully consummated until the world to come. In the Song we discover that in the allegory, which helps us grasp the story we inhabit and cultivates the longing percolating within us, giving clarity of direction. A bunch of dead ends does not make us closer to fine. What we want and need is to get in the inner chambers. We need the doors to the kingdom open to us, with a VIP entrance to the holy of holies.

Maybe it seems strange that God would use such erotic language in his Word to evoke our longing for him, to uncover what we want, and to teach us about his love for us. Is God using something that we know, like erotic love, to show the power of his love? Robert Jenson says that would be getting it backward: "Human lovers' relations to each other are recognizable in their true eroticism only by noting their analogy to an eroticism that is God's alone."[20] He uses the example of righteousness. We don't learn about it by looking at our own feeble attempts. We learn about righteousness by looking to

Christ. Our attempts only anticipate what is to come. In this way, we don't look to sex to teach us about the Song or God's eroticism, but from the Song we learn that erotic love is a gift that is to be within covenantal bounds. We see the meaningfulness in our sexuality and in the covenant of marriage. In them, we are pointing to, anticipating, a covenantal, mutual love between the incarnate Son and his people.

We don't want to miss this invitation. Sadly, some misunderstand and misuse allegory when it comes to eros. It happens when we look the wrong way, seeing the act of sex as holy. Let's not miss the beautiful picture of the triune God sending forth the Son, born of a woman, to invite us into covenantal communion. Let's not miss the blessing from Yahweh to join him in the love of the Father for the Son by the Spirit (Song 5:1). The picture has us looking to the triune God and to the Bridegroom. Much contemporary teaching on the Song and on sexuality seems driven by pragmatics and cultural ideologies of man and woman, missing the rich, divine melody of it all. We can make this kind of mistake with metaphor, typology, and allegory. We look the wrong way. We begin with ourselves to look for meaning, making the same anthropological mistake that we are still trying to recover from as a church.[21]

We continue to see this damaging mistake in Christian resources today, focusing on sex as the icon representing salvation rather than man and woman as icons representing the triune God.[22] It's tragic to see how bestselling books miss how our human nature is directed towards covenantal communion. And they miss the aim—the meaningfulness in how our bodies in masculinity and femininity are typological symbols of the redemptive covenantal union in Christ that brings us to this end. In looking the wrong way, our typology is crammed into our nature, often leading to a dangerous notion that male sexual dominance is gospel. Let's not look the wrong way. That isn't the picture in the Song at all. The bride is directing our gaze and our longings to show us what is real.

In his chambers we find true eros. We get behind the veil. We've settled for the counterfeit all too often. Wanting to be known, we end up instead losing ourselves in another. Eros is pure, holy giving of the self, involving all our senses, for the good of both. It's full, covenantal participation in union. Eros recognizes the other as gift, and in receiving that union, both persons give their freedom for the other to live in.[23] This union of lover with the beloved transcends the struggle we have in the need for both freedom and belonging, union and differentiation. Denys Turner explains, "Within erotic love I am both more me and more than me."[24]

Can we get what we want? Is this an impossible quest that leaves us in total despair? It depends on where we look for it. True eros is a divine love that we covenantally participate in. Therefore, this "more than me" language is true for created beings entering into this union, but not for the Bridegroom. He needs nothing but gives everything. He already has full freedom in belonging, differentiation of persons within oneness of essence as triune God. This is the order of love that is beckoning us. The Bridegroom is the first to love, the first to sacrifice, and the first to give. He does all this because of the love of the Father in giving him the gift of a bride. We are invited to join covenantally in the Father's love for the Son in the Spirit. This is the holy of holies—the Son came for his bride and is transforming her into his likeness so that he can usher her behind the veil. In the Song, we get a glimpse of this story of eros playing out. We get a glimpse behind the veil. If you want to know what you really want and get a picture of it that beckons all your senses, read the Song of Songs. And we see right in the beginning, the beloved bursting on the scene with the freedom to ask for what we want.

Are we courageous enough to join her? What are these kisses of his mouth that we seek? One commentator from the early church, Honorius of Autun, shares, "God kissed the Bride as it were by someone else's mouth, when formerly 'In many and various ways' he spoke 'to our fathers by the prophets' (Heb. 1:1). He kissed her, so to speak, by his own mouth when 'in these last days he spoke to them in the Son' (Heb.1:2), saying 'Peace be with you' (John 20:19).[25] He explains that it is the mouth of the Son, the "Word of the Father," that brings us the kiss of peace.[26] In this peace we are seen and secure, free to give of ourselves and receive the Son as gift in his union with us. Yet there is an already and not yet—we have a taste of these kisses, but we do not have that consummated fellowship with him in our glorification. Christ has given so much, but still we want more. We want the kisses of his mouth. Plural. Think about the best kiss you've had. It isn't an ender; it's a beginning. You hope, anyway. Kissing is playful, intimate, and erotic. We see that in the Song, and we know it in life. Audrey Hepburn is attributed, but undocumented, for saying, "I believe in kissing, kissing a lot." Can I get an amen?! Don't you see it? The lips of Jesus?

Grace flows from his lips (Ps. 45:2). And they are "lilies, dripping with flowing myrrh" (Song 5:13). The bride doesn't waste a word with her imageries and metaphors. Early in the Song, we see that she is a lily. She calls herself a "lily of the valleys" (Song 2:1), and the man responds saying she is "a lily among thorns" (Song 2:2). The royal wedding Psalm that I just quoted from begins with the introduction "For the choir director: according to 'The Lilies'. . . . A love song" (Ps. 45). I've alluded to the symbolic meaning of lilies earlier. As Havilah Dharamraj notes, Israel self-identified "as a 'lily' and a 'dove,' both familiar images in the Song." She references 4 Ezra 5:23–26, "dated to the end of the first century CE," as the first documentation of this.[27] Lilies are a metaphor for the church. In one of the searching scenes, the bride shows that she knew where to find her lover: "My love has gone down to his garden, to beds of spice, to feed in the gardens and gather lilies. I am my love's and my love is mine; he feeds among the lilies" (Song 6:2–3). He is with his people, his bride. He feeds among the lilies. So when she says that his lips *are* lilies, she is practically saying that we are on his lips! And they are dripping with myrrh, a perfume of the temple.[28]

Let's just pause and think about the intimate eros in this statement. The Shulammite talks about the lips of her lover in a way that can only be expressed through vivid and sensuous poetic images. This text is not only sharing information; it's *doing* something to us as we read it. It is practically putting us right smack on the lips of Christ! Doesn't it create a longing within you to be on those lips, to participate in this kind of beautiful eros? All our senses are drawn into it: seeing the lilies, smelling them, feeling and smelling dripping myrrh, tasting his lips. The bride gets what she wants. His lips are lilies. They are hers. They are ours, the kisses of peace, the gift of the Son, the invitation to intimacy with him. How does that change the way that we view discipleship?

SEEING CHRIST WITH HIS PEOPLE

Intimacy with Christ changes how we see, especially how we see one another. Christ's people are on his lips. Jesus bids us to consider the lilies and how they grow in the Sermon on the Mount. He says, "Not even Solomon in all his splendor was adorned like one of these" (Matt. 6:29). How glorious! Think about it. We are adorned with our Groom. We are covered with Christ! Maybe you think that I am getting carried away, connecting this language. Possibly, I am. But the same Divine Author who gives us the language of the lilies in the Song asks us to consider their splendor in talking about kingdom living—in the very context of addressing our anxieties and need for peace, or shall we say, the kisses of his mouth! In pondering the great mysteries of this language of the kisses of his mouth, St. Teresa of Avila meditates:

> It will seem to you that there are some words in the Song of Songs that could have been said in another style. In light of our dullness such an opinion doesn't surprise me. I have heard some persons say that they avoid listening to them. Oh, God help me, how great is our misery! Just as poisonous creatures turn everything they eat into poison, so do we. From favors as great as those the Lord gives us here in revealing what is possessed by the soul who Loves him and in encouraging it to speak with His Majesty and find delight in Him, we have to create fears and give opinions that manifest the small degree of love of God we have.[29]

She then captures both the reverence and freedom in discussing the words in the Song together. We cannot go wrong in pointing to the love of Christ in them, and we cannot exaggerate that love.[30] What if we do not succeed in our interpretation—of which there are layers of meaning so rich to behold? With St. Teresa, "I will consider the time well spent that I occupy in writing and reflecting upon material so divine that I haven't deserved to hear it."[31] So we are bidden to consider the lips of Jesus and the lilies of the field. And we consider one another. The woman in the Song is opening the door to the kingdom for us and beckoning us to enter in with him. She is showing us what we really want and how to ask for it. She is showing us how to talk to God and one another. Do you see that? The Song opens speaking of the king in third person. "Oh that he would kiss me with the kisses of his mouth!" (Song 1:2). And then she switches to talking directly to the king, with her request, "Take me with you—let's hurry" before immediately switching back to referring to him in the third person again, "Oh that the king would bring me to his chambers" (Song 1:4). In speaking in his absence and in his presence, she's bringing us to the entrance.

That is discipleship. It's a prayer, a proclamation, and an invitation. It's pounding on the door and holding it open for others. Desire the King of Peace. His caresses are more delightful than wine. You will feel them warm and gladden your heart (Ps. 104:15). He drank the bitterness from the cup (Matt. 26:39) and left you with only the wine's sweetness. Help others smell the fragrance of his perfume and get intoxicated together from his beds of spice (Song 5:13). Inhale his fragrance on one another, the lilies on his lips dripping with the aroma from the temple (Song 5:13). His very name—hallowed—is like perfume poured out. This is our prayer: hallowed be thy name; put us on your lips; give us peace, fullness, and unity in you, Lord.

We aren't left to guess when looking for Christ's presence. He feeds among the lilies. He is with his people. Like the bride, we listen and look (Song 2:8) together, proclaiming his approach. Now we do that in the ordinary. How absolutely absurd! All of this sounds so ethereal, so spiritual, but not like part of the material world in which we live and grocery shop. But it's both! The doors of the kingdom are open to us. The kingdom is part of our physical lives. Rowan Williams goes as far as to say:

> Only the body saves the soul. It sounds rather shocking put like that, but the point is that the soul left to itself, the inner life or whatever you want to call it, is not capable of transforming itself. It needs the gifts that only the external life can deliver: the actual events of God's action in history, heard by physical ears; the actual material fact of the meeting of believers where bread and wine are shared; the actual wonderful, disagreeable, impossible, unpredictable human beings we encounter daily, in and out of the church. Only in this setting do we become holy, and holy in a way unique to each one of us.[32]

The living God put on flesh. He took on human nature and was formed in the womb of a virgin woman. Her name was Mary. Her body was "the source for the creative act of God,"[33] with her assent (Luke 1:38). As Amy Peeler reminds us, "In the incarnation, God has deemed the female body—the impure, bleeding, female body—worthy to handle the most sacred of things, the very body of God."[34] And he gives his flesh and blood to us in the Eucharist, calling us to gather together. We remember his self-gift and look to the great feast that is to come as he nourishes us with himself. The spiritual kisses the material. By the act of his Spirit, we are lifted up, we ascend the mountain, we taste what awaits us in the holy of holies. Together.

Dallas Willard paraphrases Jesus's words in Matthew 4:17 like this: "Rethink your life in light of the fact that the kingdom of heaven is now open to all."[35] Repentance is just that. It is a rethinking, seeing what's real, turning towards it, shedding the counterfeit, and walking through the door. And let's help one another listen, see, repent, and walk. That's discipleship. That is following Jesus. Looking for that open kingdom door. Learning how to love God and one another. None of it is as abstract as we might think. Jesus makes it simple: "If you love me, you will keep my commands. And I will ask the Father, and he will give you another Counselor to be with you forever" (John 14:15–16). Obedience sounds so imposing, but it is life-giving. It's been weaponized in the world, particularly in the church. Jesus shows how the religious use obedience to close the kingdom door, piling on their self-imposed way for living while bolstering themselves: "Woe to you, scribes and Pharisees, hypocrites! You shut the door of the kingdom of heaven in people's faces. For you don't go in, and you don't allow those entering to go in" (Matt. 23:13). Keeping the commands of Jesus is simply seeing how things work in his kingdom and lead to the fullness of life. Jesus gives us an overview in the Sermon on the Mount. In it, we see the spirit of the law, the goodness of God, and the way of abundance and freedom for his people. Yet it takes a lifetime to get the whole picture into focus. He gives us the power to see and choose life over and over by his Holy Spirit. And he gives us his body, the community of the faith, to be his mouthpiece, hands, heart, core, and pinky toes. I am only a part. You are only a part. "The body is not one part but many" (1 Cor. 12:14).

We are in tune with the body when we are loving the Son. Paul tells us that if we pursue love we get all the rest (1 Cor. 13:1–14:1). We don't pursue leadership or particular giftings. We pursue the kisses of his mouth. That orients us to kingdom living, and by the power of his Spirit, we then become the kind of people who are patient, kind, rejoicing in truth, bearing all things, believing all things, hoping all things—enduring all things (1 Cor. 13:4–7). Our spiritual siblingship testifies to what we receive as gift and where we are headed. Christians are made spiritual selves in Christ only by the work of the triune God, our Creator. As a church, we are made up in Christ, so much so that we are the body of Christ.

And what happens when love is in the church? God's people delight in him together. We begin to reveal the picture of Christ's multiethnic bride as sacred siblings and advocates. And as we hear, speak, and read God's Word in community, we do so with an eschatological imagination. We are being courted and transformed by it. Church then becomes a safe place to share our stories and ask the hard questions about life, offering security as we express our doubts, protection from the harm of others, a voice to the marginalized, and humility about how much more we have to learn. We get to learn about the God of the universe, who created us to have eternal communion with him and one another. We get to not only learn about but also enter into that life of abundance. Church is the place of the open door.

Together as the church, we are the gift from the Father to the Son by the Spirit in eternity. I know, I've said that already. Once or twice. I can see it now in the reviews: "Byrd repeats herself too much." Too bad. The world needs to see a church with this vision. Right now, we don't have it all together. In most ways, we are just as messed up as everyone else. But we have something incomprehensible to our fallen minds and bodies: a love that gives us freedom in belonging. As we've discussed, it isn't the kind of freedom that we typically think about when using the word. It is a freedom to sacrifice for and love one another with all of our mind, all of our soul, and all of our strength because of our love for God. Only because he first loved us.

STATE OF THE UNION ADDRESS

Sign me up. Where do I find this community? After leaving my denomination and church, my family went looking. God is now calling us to endurance. We needed time for processing the spiritual abuse and for healing. For a while, we hid out in a small church of under fifty people and passively took it in. It was a vulnerable time. We knew the pastor and his wife, and they were aware of our situation and sensitive to it. I'm thankful for the time we had there to heal. But the big elephant in the congregation was that they were in a denomination that is being exposed for covering up hundreds of pastoral sexual abuse cases. We told them from the beginning that we would not be able to join or stay there for that reason.

We have encountered some doozies in visiting the churches in our area. And yet there was always something to learn about God there as well. We've been blessed to see God through the eyes of other ethnicities and seen congregations rise to close the food poverty gap in our city in a significant, sacrificial way. We've heard different styles of preaching and seen the widows served, missionaries helped, and churches sharing spaces for meetings to help with the needs of our community, such as addictions.

We've also worshiped where the band is so loud that we can't hear any of the unmiked voices of God's people and seen worship services turned into building fundraisers, with the widows exploited for their faithful giving. Cool people— we've seen so many cool people. We've noticed engagement is happening not by personal invitations but by joining programs. We've seen Christian Nationalism on display, with the American flag waving near the pulpit and elders rallying for local political causes. Sadly, we've also seen the gospel turned into a gimmick. One of the worst instances of this was when we drove into a church parking lot to the sound of bad nineties music blaring from the speakers. We exited our cars to Rick Astley[*] and entered the "sanctuary" to the blaring of "Gonna Make You Sweat" by C+C Music Factory, after passing a slushie

---

[*] My son, who is only familiar with Astley from "Rick rolls," was astonished that people seriously play the whole song anymore. He said, "Wait, people listen to this song for real?"

machine and fake arcade in the foyer. The "stage" was done up like a Pac Man videogame. The pastor was doing a series relating nineties videogames to the parables of Jesus—yes, quite a stretch! I don't think he grasped the point of parables. After the service, we returned to our car not knowing where to begin to process it all. My seventeen-year-old son broke the ice, "Did you notice that the worship leader began his prayer with, 'Hey God,'?" We can also close the door to the kingdom by reducing it to caricatures and ideologies.

We continued to attend that quaint, small church that meets in a converted old house for several months. The pastor sometimes quoted from Christian authors and pastors that I previously would have snubbed my nose at. I told myself that I don't care anymore. That's not true. I grimace. I have some more husks that need shucked there, so I try to keep an open mind. And I see the pastor's context—he has his finger on what is going awry in the church today. We had him and his wife over for dinner to get to know them a little, and it turns out they are in the underground too. They've seen behind the curtain. They've continuously died to their sole selves in over forty years of ministry. (Side story: His wife just so happens to have recently acquired a two-hundred pound tortoise. They have nowhere to put it so he's in a giant container in their kitchen while they figure that out. That makes them very interesting people in our book.) We continued going as we knew that more conversations needed to happen, and more worshiping together, to see if our family could thrive there following Christ. We are grateful to have another place where the pastor and his wife are happy to give us time and space for that.

I'm also trying to better listen to my now-young-adult children. They see us trying to make a church that doesn't really fit for us, or for them, work. My oldest said what I was afraid to say out loud as we were eating lunch together after the service a few weeks ago. Basically, the people there are kind but we were starved for substance. So we visited a church last Sunday that might be closer to our theological and ecclesial convictions—friendly people, more Scripture in the liturgy— but again, there were some significant issues. We are still in the developing room of waiting on God. My husband and I have a meeting with a pastor of a nearby church plant later this week. I always feel so vulnerable meeting new pastors and churches, knowing the results of the Google search and how that reduces me and my story. How will I be seen? I'm reminded to die to that. I'm reminded that I like the underground. While I listen and look for the open doors there, we will keep looking for where Christ is leading us.

Healing is happening. Throughout this time without a church home, God has given us a cloud of witnesses, those we've found in the underground as well as all those who went before us, living ordinary lives of faith and obedience before triumphing in victory to be with Christ. I hike a lot with some underground friends. Experiencing beauty with all my senses, the fresh air, the movement, baring our souls, telling our secrets, sharing our fears, daring to hope together—it's all good for my soul. The mountains hold it all. Other friends and I have a less physically demanding practice too, when the weather allows—linking our innertubes together and floating down the Potomac River. It's glorious. During both tubing and hiking, you are committed to time and fellowship without normal life interruptions. There's no quick way off a mountain or out of a river; you have to finish the course. And there's always food involved. Together we tell stories about what kind of people we are, how we've become so, what our desires are, what our disappointments are, whom we love, and how it all holds together. We are learning what matters and how to hold onto it. For me, this community of friendship and quest for beauty is crucial for healing in the face of disillusionment. God still gives his body.

The question remains before us: What have we learned about love in the church? Love is my aim now in looking. My friend Anna and I were discussing this, and she began organizing some of the themes I've been working on to help navigate what we're learning:

- Our faith is not transactional. Being loved by God is foundational. God is not going to give up on us if we make the wrong decision about what church we attend.
- God is at work in the underground. Much of what God does is invisible and outside the confines of the four walls of the church.
- We are called to beauty, and we are learning that God reveals beauty in the bride wherever we find her, even in places that may have been "cerebrally repugnant" to us before. We have come to realize that we should not put our hope in the cerebrally respectable institutions that we did before. The narrow path does not refer to correct information but obedience to love. In the real world of goodness and truth, obedience and love are not pitted against each other. Instead, understanding comes from obedience to love.

- We are the desired and beloved bride. Christ will meet us and find us where we are because he desires us and we belong to him.

- We are part of Mother Zion, received into her chambers, her citizens and her children. Belonging to her makes belonging here meaningful, not vice versa.[36] Gregory of Nyssa blew my socks off with this observation on Ecclesiastes 1:9: "God fashioned the human body and will show the resurrection at the proper time, for that which comes after the resurrection was indeed fashioned first."[37]

Knowing all this makes me closer to fine. It gives me the patience not to settle for less than the love, beauty, goodness, and truth that Christ gives.

I'm spending time in Isaiah 61 and 62, which weaves together so many of these themes, giving us the picture of the inaugurated kingdom and of what is to come. It's helping me rest in the reality of the love of the triune God for his people. Jesus began his ministry reading Isaiah 61:1–2 in the synagogue:

> The Spirit of the Lord is on me,
> because he has anointed me
> to preach good news to the poor.
> He has sent me
> to proclaim release to the captives
> and recovery of sight to the blind,
> to set free the oppressed,
> to proclaim the year of the Lord's favor. (Luke 4:18–19)

Jesus then rolls up the scroll, takes a seat with all eyes on him, and says, "Today as you listen, this Scripture has been fulfilled" (Luke 4:21). Wow! I don't think I wanted to see myself in these verses before: the poor, captive, blind, oppressed. If we go to the source in Isaiah 61, he continues to proclaim the blessing of comfort to those who mourn. Aren't these also the very ones Jesus calls blessed in the Beatitudes? I am beginning to see myself in them now and know more of his blessedness. Isaiah 61:3 says that God will "give them a crown of beauty." When we read about Zion's restoration in Isaiah 62, which is laden with echoes with the Song of Songs, we are given the promise, "You will be a glorious crown in the LORD's hand, and a royal diadem in the palm of your God's hand" (Isa. 62:3). Do you see it? *Totus Christus!* He *is* the crown of beauty, just as we are the glorious crown in Isaiah and in the Song (Song 3:11). "On that day, the LORD of Armies will become a crown of beauty and a diadem of splendor to the remnant of his people" (Isa. 28:5).

Isaiah shows our belonging, so much so that the servant song in Isaiah from which Jesus quoted, proclaiming that it is being fulfilled, tells us, "But you will be called the LORD's priests; they will speak of you as ministers of our God" (Isa. 61:6). Not just the Levites. Not just the men. Every member ministry. The priesthood of all believers, flowing from our union with Christ, mediating his blessings to one another. We are Christ to one another. That freedom in belonging is how we are to be known (Isa. 61:9). We all reveal Christ's beauty to one another.

Perhaps you have heard of the Japanese art of kintsugi. It is an art, but also a language of the value of broken pieces, the power and beauty in mending, and the story that it tells. In kintsugi, broken and cracked pieces of pottery are mended with "Japan lacquer" and mixed or dusted with precious metal powder. While we think of a repair as something functional, doing our best to hide a flaw, precious metals such as gold and silver are used in kintsugi to highlight what was broken. Artist Makoto Fujimura uses this picture, this artform, to teach us about mending from trauma. During one presentation, Fujimura holds up a twentieth century tea bowl. In presenting the kintsugi art, he speaks about how "the care of the design, the master's touch, his incredible humor is all evident" for our gaze to admire. The kintsugi art on this bowl he holds up looks like a spiderweb. What a story that tells about life! He says, "Trauma mended becomes something new." The mending itself is "a language that can speak into the divide, into the gap."[38]

Fujimura gives a brief history of the art, and he speaks about a tea master in sixteenth-century Japan who developed an art of peacemaking during a period of war by developing the art of tea. He then presents a sixteenth-century North Korean bowl, used by commoners. Upon first glance, it doesn't look significant for its beauty—just plain, dark, oddly shaped. Maybe we think of ourselves that way. Insignificant. Nothing special. Common. Oddly shaped. But the tea master saw a potential in this ordinary bowl to serve high tea to the powerful shogun. And because it was used in this way, a message was communicated. "Yes, you may be powerful, but there are more powerful things than your power. That's an artist communicating to power."[39] These ordinary bowls serve the commoners and the powerful. Fujimura says the tea master brings humility, creativity, and sanctified imagination to his art. We need this sanctified imagination when we behold one another in God's household. Then we will not want to discard the broken vessels among us as if they are merely replaceable or upgradable.

Kintsugi arose from valuing the testimony these broken pieces hold—their service over time, the hands they've been in, the humble power of their vocation, the families they belonged to, the artists who created them, and the wear and brokenness over time. Because of this, the broken pieces and cracks were viewed differently. The cracks were the horizons for beauty to emerge, "making the object that was mended more valuable than before. . . . The kintsugi bowl is far more valuable than it was before it was broken."[40] What a stark contrast to the contrived beauty I've seen visiting different churches! What a contrast to the way broken people are treated now!* It makes us wonder: What do we value? What do we see as beautiful?

There is hope in our scars. They bear testimony. They are part of a living body that is so valued by God, so much so that he took on a body of flesh so that ours would be eternally resurrected. So much so that we are considered his body. So much so that he gives us his body in sacrament for communion together in the nourishment he gives. The brokenness from others, the cracks and fault lines from our sin, the bumps on the journey of the life of faith, and the wear from

---

* If you are in a healthy church where the gospel is dazzling through the golden filling, what a blessing! I don't want my experiences and so many others' to deny that there are many good churches out there. But I am speaking into a brokenness that is saturating the Christian landscape. We have to look at it. We have to address it.

the self-sacrifice we give of our sole selves bear witness—
what a spiderweb! God doesn't want to cover over our scars
as if our stories didn't happen. They are horizons for beauty
to emerge, making something new and more valuable than
before.

Hope isn't sentimental. It bears scars. What do we learn
about hope in looking at these golden scars? Mark Labberton
discusses hope in the foreword to Fujimura's book *Culture
Care*. He begins by saying that hope "must be realistic." It
names the darkness for what it is. "If hope has not first been
silenced before the profundity of evil and loss, then such a
two-dimensional offering is more scandalous than fruitful."
He then shares that "hope . . . takes time to mature." It is like
the testimony of the golden spiderweb in the bowl Fujimura
presented. It's not merely a linear path to healing but an inter-
woven testimony of endurance. And here's the other thing:
"Hope is disruptive, counter to dominant wind patterns,
interrupting what is mapped—a crosscurrent pushing with
creativity and truth in directions that many may think neither
possible nor desirable." Hope is vulnerable. It's all the possibilities that emerge from the horizon of our scars for love, beauty,
goodness, and truth to be highlighted. He adds that it "comes
in glimpses, almost never in whole."[41]

This makes me want to add that we need to behold these
glimpses together. Kintsugi is transformational as it's seen
in community and as the pieces are made more valuable in
new use. Maybe you noticed a theme throughout this book—
one that wasn't planned—of the glorious strangeness of the
Eucharist. Who can understand it? The mystery of Christ's

body broken and transformed into Christ's body given as a love feast for his beloved. God breaks through! I am convinced that a recovery of the centering of the presence of Christ in the Eucharist in the worship service is key to mending the church. That is the horizon where we see beauty emerge, the language that speaks into the divide. It's the gold poured over the seared edges, the highlight of our hope, the truth that testifies to the evil in this world and the horror of sin. It's the history of our value, the disruption to what we think we want and need, and the testimony to where we are headed. It's the givenness of love, embraced together, around the table.

The implications from the Eucharist direct us as this act of receiving together prophecies and it preaches. In it, we all are pieces mended together into something new. Something glorious, adorned with our jewels (Isa. 61:10). And we hear and see the Lord's testimony, "My Delight Is in Her" (Isa. 62:4). We can't help but respond, "I am my love's and his desire is for me" (Song 7:10). We get a glimpse of the resplendence of Christ in one another. Our mouths are filled with laughter and our tongues with shouts of joy! For a moment, we are lifted up by the Spirit and participate together in the future breaking into the present. The doors of the kingdom are blown wide open. We gaze at the sight of the King of Peace "wearing the crown his mother placed on him on the day of his wedding—the day of his heart's rejoicing" (Song 3:11). We rise, ordinary pieces that have been kissed by the King, sent out to bless others in Christ in our ordinary lives, baring our golden scars of hope for all to see, hunting for the glimpses of beauty revealed to us in each day together. And holding open the door.

QUESTIONS FOR PERSONAL REFLECTION AND GROUP DISCUSSION

1. To tell your story more truly, which of your expectations of God, church, and discipleship need to die? What husks need to be shucked?

2. What do you think loving your enemies looks like for you now? How do you pray for them? What do you want for them? What hope is there?

3. What picture do you see of Christ through the people in your church? What do you learn of him through their unique personhood and lives? If you are not a part of a church right now, what are you learning of Christ from listening and looking for him in your family and friendships?

4. Are you uncomfortable with the erotic language in the Song? Is this a story you can inhabit? How does true eros— pure, holy giving of the self, involving all of our senses, for the good of both—transcend the struggle we have for freedom *and* belonging, union *and* differentiation? Are you courageous enough to join the bride in asking for eros?

5. What descriptions of hope stood out to you from this chapter? Do you see this in the testimony of your scars? Do you see it in the testimony of the scars of Jesus? What beauty is emerging from the cracked horizons as they are filled with Christ? How can this be a story for the church as well?

NOTES

1. Upton Sinclair, *I, Candidate for Governor: And How I Got Licked* (1935; repr., Berkeley: University of California Press, 1994), 109.

2. Dallas Willard, *The Divine Conspiracy: Rediscovering Our Hidden Life in God* (London: William Collins, 1998), 262.

3. Willard, *Divine Conspiracy*, 263.

4. Willard, *Divine Conspiracy*, 262.

5. Thanks to my friend Anna Anderson for reminding me of this, personal communication.

6. Robert Ellsberg, "Caryll Houselander," Give Us This Day (website), October 13, 2022, https://blog.giveusthisday.org/2022/10/13/caryll-house lander/

7. See Walter Brueggemann, *The Prophetic Imagination*, 40th anniversary ed. (Minneapolis: Fortress, 2018), 64.

8. T. S. Eliot's poem "Little Gidding" helps us face these existential questions by revisiting a familiar setting and seeing differently. See T. S. Eliot, *Four Quartets* (London: Faber & Faber, 1942).

9. Brueggemann, *Prophetic Imagination*, 66.

10. Brueggemann, *Prophetic Imagination*, 64–65.

11. Rowan Williams, *Where God Happens: Discovering Christ in One Another* (Boston: New Seed, 2005), 46.

12. Williams, *Where God Happens*, 47.

13. "A Grain of Wheat" from *Sounding the Seasons* by Malcolm Guite is © Malcolm Guite, 2012. Published by Canterbury Press. Used by permission. rights@hymnsam.co.uk.

14. Dietrich Bonhoeffer, *Life Together: The Classic Exploration of Christian Community* (New York: Harper & Row, 1954), 26.

15. Herman Bavinck, *Reformed Dogmatics*, vol. 3, *Sin and Salvation in Christ*, ed. John Bolt, trans. John Vriend (Grand Rapids: Baker Academic, 2006), 474.

16. Some of this language came from a personal correspondence with my friend Anna Anderson.

17. See Bonhoeffer, *Life Together*, 31.

18. See Williams, *Where God Happens*, 66.

19. See Isa. 22:13; Prov. 23:35; and Luke 12:19.

20. Robert W. Jenson, *Song of Songs* (Louisville: Westminster John Knox, 2005), 14.

21. See Aimee Byrd, *The Sexual Reformation: Recovering the Dignity and Personhood of Man and Woman* (Grand Rapids: Zondervan Reflective, 2022).

22. For example, see Aimee Byrd, "Joshua Butler, Theology in the Raw, and Looking the Wrong Way," *Aimee Byrd* (blog), March 29, 2023, https:// aimeebyrd.com/2023/03/29/joshua-butler-theology-in-the-raw-and-looking -the-wrong-way/.

23. See Denys Turner, *Eros and Allegory: Medieval Exegesis of the Song of Songs* (Kalamazoo, MI: Cistercian, 1995), 58–59.
24. Turner, *Eros*, 58.
25. Honorius of Autun, in Richard A. Norris Jr., trans. and ed., *The Song of Songs: Interpreted by Early Christian and Medieval Commentators*, The Church's Bible (Grand Rapids: Eerdmans, 2019), 24.
26. Honorius of Autun, in Norris, trans. and ed., *Song*, 24.
27. Havilah Dharamraj, *Altogether Lovely: A Thematic and Intertextual Reading of the Song of Songs* (Minneapolis: Fortress, 2018), 2–3. She footnotes 4 Ezra 5:23–26: "'My Lord, my Master,' I said, 'out of all the forests of the earth, and all their trees, you have chosen one vine; from all the lands in the whole world you have chosen one plot; and out of all the flowers in the whole world you have chosen one lily. From all the depths of the sea you have filled one stream for yourself, and of all the cities ever built you have set Zion apart as your own. From all the birds that were created you have named one dove, and from all the animals that were fashioned you have taken one sheep.'" Translated by Jeremy Knapp, https//tinyurl.com/ycs6yrfe.
28. See Davis, *Song of Songs*, 265. Myrrh was a primary ingredient in holy anointing oil.
29. St. Teresa of Avila, "Meditations on the Song of Songs," in *The Collected Works of St. Teresa of Avila*, vol. 2, trans. Kieran Kavanaugh and Otilio Rodriguez (Washington, DC: Institute of Carmelite Studies, 1980), 217.
30. See Teresa, of Avila, *Collected Works*, 218.
31. Teresa of Avila, *Collected Works*, 220.
32. Williams, *Where God Happens*, 115–16.
33. Amy Peeler, *Women and the Gender of God* (Grand Rapids: Eerdmans, 2022), 25.
34. Peeler, *Women and the Gender of God*, 61.
35. Willard, *Divine Conspiracy*, 300.
36. Much of this was lifted from a personal exchange with Anna Anderson. I told her I'm stealing it, and she said she merely used my words and regurgitated them back to me. I love her.
37. Gregory of Nyssa, *Homilies on Ecclesiastes*, Ancient Bible Commentaries in English, ed. John Litteral, trans. by Richard McCambly, (Ashland, KY: Litteral's Christian Library, 2014), 27.
38. Makoto Fujimura, "Mending Trauma" (video), Theology of Making, Fuller Studio, https://fullerstudio.fuller.edu/makoto-fujimura-on-a-theology-of-making/.
39. Fujimura, "Mending Trauma."
40. Fujimura, "Mending Trauma."
41. Mark Labberton, foreword to *Culture Care: Reconnecting with Beauty for Our Common Life*, by Makoto Fujimura (Downers Grove, IL: InterVarsity Press, 2017), 9–10.

OUTRO

A CHURCH THAT SEES

Leaving hurts.

I didn't want to leave my church. There were so many good things about it. We thought we had real community there. And we thought our elders would be able to work through their weaknesses and grow in leadership. I wanted to follow through with the hard work to get there together and come out stronger as a church family. I didn't want to be a quitter.

I also felt partly responsible—being the one who came forward with this problem. As the whole ceiling began to crumble down, it was easy to blame myself. Was I just going to stir the pot and leave them with the mess? "Troublemaker" was the gremlin in my head. But that isn't telling the story truly. That isn't how it happened. Matt was so good at presenting reality to me. Man, I appreciate that. The reality is that church officers in my own denomination were harassing, slandering, and plotting against me, and one of our own elders—the one assigned to shepherd our family—was unapologetically in this group in agreement with these men, wanting the rest of the elders to do something about my writing. The reality is that I had to stand up for myself, which is the opposite of the curated story the church tells about male protection and leadership. Something that could have been simple to address became a nightmare, and it became spiritually abusive. The reality is that the whole thing revealed underlying beliefs about women, power, and constructed, unbiblical systems. The problem wasn't merely one incident or one case handled badly; it was a whole system of belief. The reality is that many saw this, yet I was left carrying all the shame. This isn't what church should be. Where was love? Where was Christ?

My elders tried, which persuaded me to stay much longer than I should have. It's so difficult when you can see the good peeking through, when you and your family are invested—not only in the church but in the relationships—and when you are trying so hard to make sense of what is happening to you. Every attempt to communicate and move forward became more painful than the last. But the church leaders agreed to hire a professional therapist who specialized in spiritual abuse for me to have a session with, for them to work with as they felt needed, and for all of us to come together for a joint session. At the end of my personal session, the psychiatrist said something clarifying: "Why do you think you need to be a missionary in your own church?" I couldn't get that question out of my head. This isn't how it is supposed to be. I need a church where it is safe to learn, contribute, question, and grow together. Instead, I had been functioning like a missionary. What does that say about those who are to shepherd my family? And how we shepherd one another? How did this happen? That could be another book, but this one is about rising from what did happen.

Before our family left our church and denomination, the question I kept asking myself about if and when to leave was this: *Are we safe here?* Every time I asked myself that question, the answer kept being a resounding no. Then I realized how messed up and disoriented I was to be asking this question. Why am I not asking: *Is our family flourishing here?* And *are we in a community that joins, directs, and participates with us in communion with the triune God and one another?* Church isn't supposed to be the mission field.

What kind of church we want to be a part of connects with what we think discipleship is. I was in that church because I thought discipleship began with having the right doctrine. I thought knowing the right things about God led to godliness. It was shocking to me to see the complete lack of spiritual maturity in so many leaders—not only the ones harassing me but in the many who gave them safe passage, and even in those who were trying to do something about it. It was painful to see the lack of spiritual maturity of so many in the church. This caused much disillusionment. I kept looking to leaders, fellow congregants, friends, and the very system offered to address it, expecting them to give me something that they just did not have.

This outro was supposed to be an appendix titled "When to Leave Your Church." But after writing the book, it became clearer to me that this asks a question I cannot answer for you. We want things to work out at our churches. We want growth for everyone. We know there will be conflict. We know the church is made up of people God is still working on. Including ourselves. People who will fail God and us. People who might harm us.

We want to be the type of people who persevere in love. Love is a must. Sometimes we've been swimming in the water so long that we don't realize the counterfeit loves that take real love's place.

Leaving can be necessary. Sometimes it is best to move on. As I said in the last chapter, our faith is not transactional. Being loved by God is foundational. God is not going to give up on us if we make the wrong decision about what church we attend. There are a number of reasons to leave a church and a lot of gray areas where God may be calling you to stay. Prayer and wise friendships are key. No one should stick around in abusive cultures, under bad theology, or where their personhood is diminished because of sex, ethnicity, class, age, and the like. And I don't mean only if it's happening to you. If you stay because you aren't affected while others are harmed, you are allowing safe passage for cruelty and the dehumanization of Christ's bride. You legitimize it. Ask yourself, what benefit am I getting at the cost of the personhood of my siblings and partners in Christ? Am I their partner in affliction, kingdom, and endurance here?

Rather than get into all the reasons to leave a church, which are often evident, let's circle back to the scars of our disillusionment and look for the beauty in the mending, the beauty of a church in transition as a whole. What kind of church do we want to be a part of? We began this book with the notion that Christ uses our disillusionment as a tool to direct us to him, to show himself to us. He reveals the counterfeit belonging we were trying to find satisfaction in, which is an act of his grace. He brings our broken pieces together with the broken body of Christ given for us, his blood like kintsugi gold, in which the mending is participation in and beholding of the great wonder of his unitive love.

Disillusionment about who Christ is and what makes up his church was a struggle with his earliest disciples. The Bible is full of disillusioned disciples—while they are with Jesus! In John 6:53–68, Jesus says, "Truly I tell you, unless you eat the flesh of the Son of Man and drink his blood, you do not have life in yourselves," (v. 53) and how many disciples deserted him because it was too hard to understand? That passage organically unfolded before us in each subsequent chapter of this book. The mystery of it becomes greater in its unfolding, not lessened. But we see his closest disciples disillusioned *after* the resurrection.

Mary Magdalene, the first Jesus appears to, does not recognize him initially (John 20:14). When he reveals himself to her, he warns her that it is not yet the time she is hoping for, where she can cling to him in the house of Zion (Song 3:4). But he commissions her to tell the disciples of his resurrection (John 20:17–18).

Thomas is not with the others when Christ first appears to them on that glorious Sunday of the resurrection. Why is he absent, we may wonder?[1] Is that a sign of his disillusionment? What's a disciple to do now that Christ is gone? What else does he have to do with these people? When the others find Thomas and tell this "one of the twelve" about how they have "seen the Lord," he isn't buying it. He uses a strong word. He will *never* believe—if he doesn't see the scars. As a matter of fact, he's going to need to touch them too (John 20:24–25). A full week goes by, and Jesus appears to them again on the following Sunday. Thomas is around this time. And behold, Jesus addresses his disillusionment straight on, appearing and inviting him to look at and touch his scars and believe (John 20:26–27).

The third time Jesus appears to the disciples, they were fishing through the night. That is concrete for them. Think about it. What are they to do with this encounter with the risen Christ, having breathed on them to receive the Holy Spirit with the power to forgive sins (John 20:21)? That is some disorienting stuff. Something is happening, but meanwhile, the regular duties of life are before them. In this third encounter, we see more disillusionment. The disciples don't recognize him at first. Don't you think at this point, having seen their beloved risen from the grave, they would be looking for him in expectation? I love how Jesus approaches them in the morning, beginning his witty and comedic observation about their lack of any fish with the greeting "friends" (21:4–5). This time he deals with Peter's disillusionment. That heavy shame he was walking with for denying him three times in his worst hour. The gaze of Jesus when they met eyes the third time he denied him at the rooster's crow (Luke 22:61), who can bear it? And Jesus is looking at Peter again, directing Peter to his love, giving Peter the invitation to proclaim that love to him, thrice, and commissioning him to feed his sheep and follow him (John 21:15–19). This is the kind of God Peter could never have imagined. This is the kind of love he needs.

Cleopas and another disciple were walking to Emmaus when they did not recognize Jesus walking beside them. Jesus speaks with them as they discuss the emotional and bewildering news of his death and reported resurrection (Luke 24:16). Those women astound the disciples with the news. We've already spent time with these disciples, but Jesus meets their disillusionment by giving them eyes to find him in the reading of the Scriptures and in the bread and the wine—Christ with us. Do you see how we are learning about church and discipleship as Jesus meets his disciples' disillusionment?

Disillusionment appears again in the giving of the Great Commission: "All authority has been given to me in heaven and on earth. Go, therefore, and make disciples of all nations, baptizing them in the name of the Father and of the Son and of the Holy Spirit, teaching them to observe everything I have commanded you. And remember, I am with you always, to the end of the age" (Matt. 28:18–20). We read in this account that some of the eleven disciples, who were following the directions Jesus gave them to travel to a mountain in Galilee, beholding and worshiping the resurrected Christ at their destination, doubted (Matt. 28:17). Some *still* doubted. Can this really be real? I bet they were beat up about that doubt. But Jesus turns them into disciple makers.

Who else is a disciple except someone who recognizes and walks with Jesus? Dallas Willard breaks it down: "Discipleship is a life of learning from Jesus Christ how to live in the Kingdom of God now, as he himself did."[2] Jesus opens the door, helps us see reality through our disillusionment, and bids us to fullness of life in his kingdom. We go with him.

GIVE US SIGHT AND RECOGNITION; LORD, OPEN THE DOOR

Christ is revealing much to his church in all the disillusionment around us. He is showing us what is real. A lot of what we thought was "good Christianity" isn't real. A lot of what we put our hope in wasn't real. Heck, a lot of what is displayed and enacted as Christian leadership is not real. Our own sense of self can be an illusion. Let's be a church that helps one another lay it all down for the glorious real thing. Christ's coming to meet us at the underground is very real. Let's talk about being in a church that sees. Let that be our prayer.

The church is full of disillusionment. Like his original disciples, we are missing Christ. He's inviting us to look at his scars and the story they tell. We need a church that sees . . .

A church that sees what's real. A church that sees the brokenness but is looking at the edges as horizons of beauty where Christ works. What story is being told about the church? Is she curated? Is she protective and defensive? Is she accessible? Is she repentant? We can be honest about our doubts, failures, and shame because we know that Christ sees and has poured out his precious blood all over those edges, highlighting the mending work, filling us with himself, bringing us to greater joy and value than we ever imagined. We can be partners in affliction, kingdom, and endurance when we see what is real together.

A church that sees Christ. What story is being told about who God is and whom he loves? Is the church helping us see Christ with us? In us? In you? In me? In his Word and sacraments? In our ancient creeds? Are we looking for him? Are we confessing him? Are we asking him to reveal himself in these ways? Are we practicing his presence together?[3] Do we see the fruits of spiritual maturity happening? A basic mission of the church is to make disciples. What discipleship making do you see in your church? Are people growing in Christ and continuously walking with him together? He promises to be with us. This is a Trinitarian love that joins with the Father, by the Spirit, in love for the Son.

A church that sees Christ in you. Are you seen? Are you known? Who has helped you tell your story truly? Who stayed in the room with you when the difficult stories came out? Who has lamented with you and helped you imagine the joy of *with*ness through it? What is the culture of a church that sees Christ in you—one fueled by fear and shame or by freedom in belonging? Are you seen as an invaluable part of the body of Christ, helping others see the whole picture of Christ more clearly? Do others help you see Christ in yourself? In this way, do they also help you die to your sole self so that you can tell your story more truly? Are you invested in, cared for, invited to contribute where the Spirit directs? Would they extend any personal invitations to get to know you if you don't join one of their programs? Would they miss you in your absence?

A church that sees Christ in the earthly otherness of every other. What stories are being told about the people inside and outside the church? Do we see the need of every person there to show us what we do not see of Christ? And of his bride? Or are there only a number of "important" people carrying the church? Would your neighbor feel welcome and wanted in your church? Would someone who is not in your neighborhood, not your ethnicity, or not in your social class feel welcome? That kind of church hangs out in the underground, expectantly looking for resurrections. The people there are more valued than the institution, denomination, and procedures. Do we see the earthly story of each other, woven with our own stories, giving our stories new light in the reality and beauty of the gospel? This church encourages obedience to the Word because it opens the kingdom door and shows the way we walk in the fullness of life. It is a church where repentance comes naturally because we behold the beauty of Christ together and don't hold our shortcomings over one another. In ministry to one another, we will gently correct[4] one another in the context of love and desire to keep us walking together with Jesus. In this way, it is also a church that seeks the voices of the marginalized and rebukes abuses of power.

A church that sees beauty, goodness, and truth. We sing together because of joy and gratitude. We lament together because faith meets us at the abyss. We pray together because we really believe that we are also spiritual beings, communing with Christ, who gives. We expect resurrection together because we are a body that is rebirthed and fruit producing through death. We preach the Word to one another because Christ is living and active in it. We baptize because Christ leads us together out of the Red Sea to living waters and because we belong to him in his death and resurrection in the name of the Father, the Son, and the Holy Spirit. We eat together in expectation of Christ joining us at the table, practicing for that Great Feast that we will share in the new heaven and new earth. We gather to receive the Eucharist because Christ is present, giving himself to us, in a mysterious and powerful way. This is the invitation into the real. Our participation in it is practice for eternity. We are sent out with this truth—Christ with us—as he continues to form us into his likeness in earthly otherness together. I believe that on the Great Day, when he returns for his bride to consummate his love, we too will be raised with the testimony of our scars, testifying to the hope that taught us how to see beauty, how to love, and how to walk in goodness together.

Let's pray for the church Christ is preparing for himself.

Let's pray to be a part of this and listen and look for the open doors whether in the church we are a part of or in looking for a better fit. Don't settle for something that calls itself church and fails to tell you the true story of who you are in Christ. Leaders, lead the way in helping us see and navigate what's real. Let's develop our love for God together because we aren't supposed to do it alone. Let's integrate our lives. Let's practice heaven so that we are trained, body and soul, when we get there. Give us sight and recognition, Lord. Open the door.

NOTES

1. See Claude R. Alexander Jr., *Becoming the Church: God's People in Purpose and Power* (Downers Grove, IL: InterVarsity Press, 2022), 3–6. The beginning of this book also highlighted to me how disillusioned the disciples were after the resurrection.

2. Dallas Willard, *The Great Omission: Reclaiming Jesus's Essential Teachings on Discipleship* (New York: HarperOne, 2006), 62.

3. A bit borrowed from Brother Lawrence's work titled, *The Practice of the Presence of God*, trans. Marshall Davis (n.p.: Marshall Davis, 2013).

4. See Jim Wilder and Michel Hendricks, *The Other Half of Church: Christian Community, Brain Science, and Overcoming Spiritual Stagnation* (Chicago: Moody, 2020), 127–54.

ACKNOWLEDGMENTS

To the leaders in the church who mocked me, harassed me, plotted against me. To those who silently lurked, returning for another hit of dopamine, salivating as you scrolled, smiling to see a sister slandered and slaughtered. To the maniacal meme makers, the anonymous account agitators, and the miscellaneous misogynists. To the doomsday YouTube prophets and the preachers of God's perfect hatred toward people like me. To the reputation destroyers and the blacklisters. To the authoritative assemblies who denied me witness, agency, care, and personhood. To my friends who betrayed me, all the while trying to convince me to accept this. To the ones who offered me private messages of encouragement but who did not speak on my behalf before others. To those who tried to advocate for me but found they were lacking in sight and tools for ministry toward the ones harmed by their own system, denomination, and theology. To those who see how wrong it all was but looked away because they didn't want to sacrifice their own comfort and benefits. To those who continue, business as usual.

You helped me see the underground. I must name what you did as wrong, cruel, and misguided. But I am glad I now see what's real. Maybe I'm one of those who needed such a severe mercy to die to my sole self. I'm learning that dying to self is a daily, hourly, minutely practice that I am still all too weak in. I do hope to see you in the underground one day. May you be led to repentance, and may we look at all the husks we shed in wonder and rejoice at it all together.

To those who welcomed me in the underground, who saw me, nurtured me, listened to me endlessly try to make sense of what was happening, who filled my pain with the golden kintsugi of Christ's love, admiring the art of our scars together and the powerful testimony they told, thank you. To my fellow hiking companions and saunterers, Anna Anderson, Dana Tuttle, and Aimee Deweese, thanks for looking for beauty with me. We've shed a lot of husks together and unearthed many treasures. To my long-distance encouragers and underground queens, Valerie Hobbs and Rachel Miller. To mine and Matt's Potomac River "Clinch" floating friends, who held my story with me: Shannan, Jim, John, Dave, and Jolie. And to Traci, whom we still need to get on the river. We've all faced disillusionment together. What an honor it has been sharing our earthly otherness with one another.

Thank you to the friends who gave their blessings to share their stories in this book. I used different names to protect privacy. And thank you to my other additional readers of the manuscript while in progress: Anna Anderson, Jeff Hutchinson, and my husband, Matt. That last guy really held me together through it all—I love you, Matt.

Thank you to Rob Downs and Jeff McCann for pastoring churches that functioned as weigh stations where our family could heal in transition.

I want to thank my agent, Don Gates, for directing me to speak into this disillusionment that so many are experiencing in the church and for navigating a home for the book. And once again, it was a pleasure to work with the folks at Zondervan. I've grown as a writer through working with Katya Covrett and value the friendship that has emerged from it. Thank you, Matt Estel, for strengthening the manuscript and for pushing me to further clarity in my writing. And working with Alexis De Weese a second time increases my joy in publishing. Thank you, along with the rest of the Zondervan team, for all you put into this—and into me.

And thank you to my readers, who have traversed through your own disillusionment looking for what is real and what is beautiful. May this book serve as a partner in affliction, kingdom, and endurance.